The Spirit Searches Everything

Cowley Publications is a ministry of the brothers of the Society of Saint John the Evangelist, a monastic order in the Episcopal Church. Our mission is to provide books and resources for those seeking spiritual and theological formation. Cowley Publications is committed to developing a new generation of writers and teachers who will encourage people to think and pray in new ways about spirituality, reconciliation, and the future.

The Spirit
Searches Everything

❧

Keeping Life's Questions

Frederick Borsch

Cowley Publications
Cambridge, Massachusetts

Published in the United States of America by Cowley Publications, a division of the Society of Saint John the Evangelist. No portion of this book may be reproduced, stored in or introduced into a retrieval system, or transmitted, in any form or by any means—including photocopying—without the prior written permission of Cowley Publications, except in the case of brief quotations embedded in critical articles and reviews.

Library of Congress Cataloging-in-Publication Data:

Borsch, Frederick Houk.
    The Spirit searches everything : keeping life's questions / Frederick Borsch.
    p. cm.
Includes bibliographical references (p.   ).
    ISBN13: 978-1-56101-226-8
    ISBN: 1-56101-226-2 (pbk. : alk. paper) 1. Spirituality—Episcopal Church.
2. Christian life—Episcopal authors. 3. Borsch, Frederick Houk. I. Title.

BV4501.3.B665 2005
248.4'82—dc22
                                                                2005008287

Scripture quotations are taken from *The New Revised Standard Version of the Bible,* © 1989, by the Division of Christian Education of the National Council of the Churches of Christ in the United States of America. Used by permission.

From *House of Light* by Mary Oliver
Copyright © 1990 by Mary Oliver
Reprinted by permission of Beacon Press, Boston

Excerpt from "Aubade" from *Collected Poems* by Philip Larkin. Copyright © 1988, 2003 by the Estate of Philip Larkin. Reprinted by permission of Farrar, Straus and Giroux, LLC.

Cover design: Gary Ragalia
Text design: Lindy Gifford

This book was printed in the United States of America on acid-free paper.
Second Printing

Cowley Publications
4 Brattle Street
Cambridge, Massachusetts 02138
800-225-1534 • www.cowley.org

Preface

How is it that we not only think but also think about ourselves thinking and are aware of ourselves and the world about us? Is this awareness alone in the universe? Or is it in some way related to a quality fundamental to creation? Why is there not nothing? What is the universe made of? How does it run itself? Could there be a Spirit of life that cares for us? How might we experience this? Why is there so much evil, wrong, and suffering in the world?

Are we for anything? Can our lives be said to have meaning? What is a good life? How can we best live together? Why am I so often restless and unsatisfied? What is it that I long for? What happens to us at death?

These are questions I have found myself asking ever since I remember myself. And I have recognized them to be questions not just about me but about all of us. I once taught a seminar in which a group of university students met with me over a period of years to talk about these issues. Coming from different religious backgrounds, they were bright and vibrant and full of their own ideas and wondering. They decided to call our time together "Big Questions." We laughed at our audacity and asked what could be the biggest question of all: whether there was any point in asking our questions. We decided that we had to

1

go on asking and exploring. More than *homo sapiens*—humans knowing, we are humans questioning—*homo quaerens.*

That exploration does not happen apart from the stories of our lives. "At its heart," Frederick Buechner once observed, "most theology, like most fiction, is essentially autobiography. Aquinas, Calvin, Barth, Tillich, working out their systems in their own ways and in their own language, are all telling us the stories of their lives, and if you press them far enough, even at their most cerebral and forbidding, you find an experience of flesh and blood, a human face smiling or frowning or weeping or covering its eyes before something that happened once."

Here are some of my questions and reflections, some of my hints and hopes, smiles and frowns, tears and stories that I hope might bring on yours as well.

One ❈ With Self Aware

In and Out of Body

I have had an out-of-body experience. When I was thirty-five and teaching at a theological school just north of Chicago, and also the father of three little boys, I began having feelings of fatigue and aching in my legs. The pain occurred after I had lectured for an hour or so or had been to a museum or the like. It was diagnosed as a problem resulting from cracked vertebrae in my lower spine. The doctor could not say what caused it. When I was an adventurous five-year-old, I had taken my picnic lunch high up into a box elder tree and then managed to slip and fall some forty feet to the ground. Luckily I only broke an arm and a leg, though I'm sure I terrified my parents. Maybe, Dr. Sweeney wondered, the damage had begun with that fall.

We tried special stockings, corsets, and exercises. Sometimes I had to lie down for hours to recover from the pain that made me cranky and upset. Pain medication did not seem to touch the aching, which now was in my back as well. The only thing that gave my some relief was liquor, and I'm surprised I did not become an alcoholic.

Finally, it was decided that I should undergo an operation for a spinal fusion. A piece of ileum bone would be taken from my pelvis and encouraged to fuse together with the vertebrae. This work of carpentry

3

was complicated and lasted many hours. Later that night my blood pressure dropped dramatically. Sometime after midnight the surgeon and my wife, Barbara, were summoned back to the hospital. I have no specific understanding of what was done (presumably I was given more blood and oxygen), but several days later I realized that I had an uncanny memory of watching the doctor and my horizontal self from up above in a corner of the room. Dr. Sweeney seemed rather relaxed, which was comforting. I could not see the whole room, but I could hear him talking to someone else who was there.

This experience happened only once, and I don't really put a lot of stock in such things. Or, let me put it this way: I am on guard. Like Martin Luther, who was concerned about too much fascination with miracles, I am wary that interest in matters that smack of extrasensory perceptions and the like could deflect attention from the world in which we live and from the wonder and challenge of creation. Moreover, reasonable attempts have been made to explain near-death, out-of-body experiences in neurophysiological terms. Anesthetics or lack of oxygen can cause dramatically altered brain states and perhaps bring about such unusual sensations and phenomena.

What the experience did lead me to do, however, was to reflect on the astounding human capacity to have an awareness of self. There I was, even in my severely depleted state, somehow vaguely aware of myself and my condition. What makes human life seem so extraordinary is not only that we have consciousness of what is going on around us but also that we can be conscious of our consciousness. We can think about ourselves thinking and reflect on who we are. I do so as I write this. I am in a kind of dialogue with myself, observing, sometimes questioning and responding. I can imagine that you are, too, as you read this. It is this capacity that also enables humans to become aware of others and to be individuals, so that we can form friendships and live in community. It is our self-awareness that enables us to imagine past and future; to shape language and story; to be creative, self-critical, and responsible; and to have compassion and loves. Such awareness becomes more than consciousness—or is a higher form of consciousness—because we may also have some awareness of the activity of our unconscious selves. We may have some awareness that we have motivating forces within us that we cannot fully lift to consciousness. We are aware of feelings and emotions. We may be mindful of autonomous capacities for breathing and for turning bits of light on our retinas into sight, even if we do not understand how they work. We can be aware of our capacities for riding a bicycle, driving a car, or learning a language, even when we are not thinking much about them. Our bodies are included in our awareness. We can have a sense of our presence in relationship with others.

Much of the time we are not so reflective about ourselves. We do not always think about ourselves thinking in such ways. Consciousness, moreover, largely abandons us when we fall asleep, only to reappear when we wake in the morning with perhaps some reminiscences of dreaming. Yet, although we are not always aware of our awareness, one may also come to feel that such awareness of self is always there to some degree—that it never completely goes away.

Complex and Surprising

Think about it! And as soon as we do, our sense of both awe and curiosity increases. The three pounds of human brain, with its labyrinthine folds and interrelated parts, have as many as one hundred billion nerve cells, or neurons. With their densely branching dendrites, there are trillions of synapses, or junction points. In the early years of life, hundreds of thousands of new synapses are being formed every second. It may seem that the universe is huge, but every human brain has more possible neural relationships than there are particles in the universe. Something so complex is bound to be full of mysteries and surprises. From the brain emerge many different forms of mental activity.

Many people have asked, What is the relationship between the physical brain and our mental activities? We may imagine this to be something like a switchboard and a switchboard operator, although it is obviously much more than that—not least in the complexity of the interactivity. Though we may understand the mental to be wholly dependent on the physical, it also seems to become something more in the mutually reciprocal relationships between the neural and mental processes. These are something like a series of diverse but integrated and often overlapping computation and remembering modules doing parallel processing. The networks and hierarchies of the brain and mental activities then organize and direct the parts so that what is taking place is more than just a sum of the neural functions.

We may well be astounded by the capability of the brain/mind to see as it takes in the sensory data that comes to it. I could, for example, be watching a mountain goat move up a rocky ledge. The photons of the light I *see* fall on the proteins at the back of my eye. These bend and stretch as the rods and cones of my retinas break the data into pixels, or a series of dots. Then, using its stereoscopic vision, the brain/mind applies complex rules and algorithms in order to distinguish concave surfaces from convex ones, for interpreting changes in intensity of motion, along with many other interpretative operations. A few moments later I may shut my eyes and yet still be able to *see* in my mind the scene of the mountainside with the goat.

This seems amazing, but it is not all that is happening. At the same time I could be thinking about how I want to become a better photographer and whom I might talk to about buying a new camera. Still at the same time I may have a vague feeling of happiness and be wondering why this is so. Oh, I forgot to mention that I am also walking and, of course, breathing and fooling with the strap of the camera in my hand. Long spindle cells are lighting up in various parts of the brain, sending signals in the form of feelings as well as in the form of ideas and thoughts.

At least four levels of mental activity can be distinguished while I do all this. Autonomous activities, for instance, regulate my blood pressure and do the combinational work that enables me to see. Dependent as I am on these autonomous systems, I cannot bring them into consciousness or control them. At another level is the breathing and walking that I do without thinking about them, but that I can become aware of and direct in different ways if I choose to do so. Walking is actually a learned activity—one that, after I broke my leg in that fall from the tree, I had to relearn. But such activities, once learned, can also be done without thinking about them. Indeed, it is a highly valuable aspect of brain activity that skills once learned (walking, riding a bicycle) can be relegated, as it were, to a kind of unconsciousness so that the brain and mind can be free to do other things—to window shop, for example, or watch for traffic signals and pedestrians.

Humans have a number of these functions in common with other animals. They are sometimes identified as parts of the lower, or reptilian, brain, with the mammalian brain parts having developed over them. Out of that mammalian brain, and then in far more developed ways through the human neocortex, appears a consciousness of what is happening. We have this consciousness much of our waking time, although it is complex and difficult to describe. It is what we take in with our senses and *picture* as we construct a present scene. In a more complicated way, it is the capacity to use forms of memory to hold what we perceive to be happening in a kind of immediately remembered present. We could call this primary consciousness, and at least a good part of this form of consciousness is shared with other animals. If my dog, Sydney, were with me, he, too, could see the mountain goat and might even consider trying to chase it.

Although I am not prepared to deny sweet Sydney some aspect of self-awareness, what he does not have is my further capacity to reflect on all that is happening, to consider the self as a potentially better photographer, and to wonder about the feeling of happiness. I think, for instance, of the potentials of the subjunctive mood of speech (I *might* buy a new camera) that allow me the nuances of supposition, desire, and possibility. And, as I reflect in this way, I become even more aware of myself in relation to the scene. I ask why I chose this scene to describe. I can marvel at the capacity to symbolize: the rocky ledge, I may imagine, represents danger. I can perform more complicated mental *games*. I am also able, for instance, to generalize from an individual to a class of them, and then go the other way around. A whole family of jokes depends on our ability to appreciate the difference: "Twice a day," someone might inform us, "a mountain goat falls off a rocky ledge." We understand that this observation refers to the average slippage of a large number of mountain goats, but the comic response is, "Oh, that poor goat!"

Then consider the sophisticated metaphorical gymnastics that go into the capacity to understand (to *get*) the Peanuts comic strip that features Charlie Brown and Linus on a cruise ship. Charlie explains to Linus that some of the passengers prefer to position their deck chairs looking forward to see where they are going, while other passengers place their chairs in the direction of the stern to see where they have been. As Linus tries to puzzle out what all this might mean regarding one's philosophy of life, Charlie explains that his own dilemma is that he cannot figure out how to unfold his deck chair.

I am interested, too, in what you, dear reader, think of this story. I could go further and wonder what you think of me for telling it, and, as I try to take all this in, I realize that such thinking processes, emotions, and imaginings are dependent on my physical brain and its multicompetent systems. But a lot more than physical brain activities seems to be happening.

How can this be? From the spatial brain comes consciousness that does not seem to occupy space. From the gelatinous tissue and buzzing of neurons arises an activity, such as thinking about buying a new camera, that is nonphysical. In her inimitable way, Emily Dickinson reflected on the brain's capacity to take in the world (perhaps God, too) and be a self in the world in which it exists.

> The brain—is wider than the Sky—
> For—put them side by side—
> The one the other will contain
> With ease—and You—beside.

Other organs of the body, though also made of organic matter, do not have this manner of consciousness. Machines do not have consciousness. We may think that someday they will, but we have no idea how that may come about because we do not understand how such consciousness comes about. Although we know we have minds and we realize brains are necessary for the mind to exist, we still have not figured out what it is about brains that brings consciousness into being. A great deal of study continues to be done, and some scientists and philosophers are sure we will eventually come to understand consciousness, or at least all its physical characteristics. Others are less sure, and wonder if our intelligence is structured in such a way that we will never know. How, among other things, can we best think *about* what we are thinking *with*? Can we do this in any satisfactory way at all?

And yet consciousness is basic enough that it is constantly being reproduced. Sydney and other animals have forms of it, and each new life, I realize, starts from the coming together of cells from parents to form a zygote that becomes a tiny embryo. The genes in these cells are able to replicate consciousness. The minute bits, linked on the double spirals of genetic coding, carry the information that grows a brain and reproduces consciousness. In that sense the coding *understands* how consciousness comes about, even if we do not.

Then we humans add a highly developed consciousness of consciousness and awareness of self. From all the neurons, axons, and synapses of the brain, and out of different aspects of consciousness, arises this genie of awareness that I call *myself*. We have, as it were, access to our consciousness, and with it our questionings and wonderings.

When, How, and Why?

When and how and why did the capacity for self-awareness develop? When, in other words, did prehuman creatures become human? Did they do so slowly and perhaps unevenly over many generations as the upper and frontal parts of the brain grew larger? As more long spindle cells (distinctive in human beings and to a much lesser degree in apes) grew, did the brain begin to *talk* within itself in new ways? Or was it more like a *click*, with a switch being thrown once the human brain was fully formed? To suggest one possibility, was there a physiological change in the *corpus callosum*, a central communications conduit that allowed a new form of communication between the hemispheres of the brain?

Given the many aspects of brain activity, one can imagine that the evolutionary development of the higher form of consciousness was quite complex. Consciousness and awareness, although they are dependent on some parts of the brain more than others, seem to be fairly well distributed in the brain. They are more a function of the whole brain than of one specific center. They result from a massive amount of signaling back and forth in a dense network of myriad systems. A number of these systems have memory capacities. With different jobs to do, they act reciprocally and are highly integrated. They work in parallel, and many times are able to back each other up by taking over the other's functions.

Once again I fall asleep. Unconsciousness is punctuated by fleeting images, seemingly random, unorganized flashes of memory. Then the mind awakes and reorganizes itself. I reappear to myself. But who has done the organizing?

The analogy of switching on a complex computer is sometimes used, but it is not very apt. Computers can do some things more quickly and efficiently than the brain, but the human brain is far more flexible and adaptive. It works by estimation and approximation instead of a strict linear logic. That enables the brain to guess and imagine as it signals back and forth within itself. No analogy can encompass the brain's complexity, but a better one would be a large orchestra with its many independent performers. Each is doing its own thing in the orchestra, but also listening to one another and so becoming able to interact and play together. In this analogy there is no conductor. The whole orchestra, like the whole brain, makes the music, resulting in the best overall coordination and direction the parts can muster.

The developing physical and mental capacities for memory would have been vital for the emergence of a sense of time and the formation of language crucial to awareness. Surely this must have evolved over generations, although one can still imagine awareness coming about in a relatively short period of biological time as these skills and abilities were exercised and then passed on.

Consciousness has obvious purposes and rewards that enable species to realize what is happening around them, to fashion strategies for dealing with danger, obtaining food and sex, and so forth. As humans engaged in more complex activities of hunting and cultivating, one can see how those with higher consciousness would have been rewarded.

They would have been better able to cope and strategize. Evolution would have *selected* more and more of those who had their kinds of brains in order to pass on their genes for conscious intelligence to the next generation.

The value of the higher consciousness of self-awareness, however, is not so obvious. Although nature, we have come to learn, rarely does something for nothing, some evolutionary biologists have wondered if self-awareness could be just a spin-off of the complex forms of intelligence we have been describing. Stephen Jay Gould thought self-awareness to be "a glorious accident." Accident or not, one can imagine it developing along with cunning, creating a kind of cognitive arms race in which humans found it helpful, in the name of survival, to be able to imagine what another person might be thinking, then to think what the other might be thinking oneself thinking, then to think about what the other is thinking about what one is thinking the other is thinking. That may sound complicated, but people making a business deal manage to do it often enough. So do couples out on a date.

Whatever its origins, self-awareness has not always been experienced as a blessing. The story in the Book of Genesis about Adam and Eve eating of the fruit from the tree that brings the knowledge of good and evil alludes to another side of self-awareness:

> And the LORD God commanded the man, "You may freely eat of every tree of the garden; but of the tree of the knowledge of good and evil you shall not eat, for in the day that you eat of it you shall die." . . .
>
> Now the serpent was more crafty than any other wild animal that the LORD God had made. He said to the woman, "Did God say, 'You shall not eat from any tree in the garden'?" The woman said to the serpent, "We may eat of the fruit of the trees in the garden; but God said, 'You shall not eat of the fruit of the tree that is in the middle of the garden, nor shall you touch it, or you shall die.'" But the serpent said to the woman, "You will not die; for God knows that when

you eat of it your eyes will be opened, and you will be like
God, knowing good and evil." So when the woman saw that
the tree was good for food, and that it was a delight to the
eyes, and that the tree was to be desired to make one wise,
she took of its fruit and ate; and she also gave some to her
husband, who was with her, and he ate. Then the eyes of
both were opened, and they knew that they were naked; and
they sewed fig leaves together and made loincloths for themselves. (Genesis 2:16–17, 3:1–7)

Adam and Eve ate of the forbidden fruit and "then their eyes were
opened." They came to see themselves as actors and participants as they
thought about who they were and what they were doing. Among other
things, "they knew that they were naked," and the story also suggests
an explanation for the shame and guilt that can accompany the awareness of sexuality.

Awareness of self as a responsible actor, having potential for accomplishments and yet many limitations, and knowing dreams as well as fail-
ures and mortality, can, at least from time to time, be experienced as a
burden from which one would wish to escape. More than a few artists and
philosophers have interpreted awareness as an accident, a sometimes
lonely and depressing one at that, marooning humans in a hostile universe.
Efforts to escape can lead to destructive behaviors with alcohol, drugs,
high speed in cars, and the like. Some have wondered if the burdensome
aspects of self-awareness might eventually doom the whole human species,
as happens on an individual level with the victims of suicide.

Had we the chance, we might think of shouting to our predecessor
Adams and Eves: *No, don't do it. Don't eat of the tree and gain such understanding and awareness. Just go on living without thinking about it.* Would
it not be a kind of paradise to live without such awareness? Yet, we realize, it is this awareness that makes them and us fully human.

Language and Story

Adam and Eve tell God what happened to them. "The woman whom you gave to be with me, she gave me the fruit from the tree, and I ate" (Genesis 3:12). "The serpent tricked me," the woman explains, "and I ate" (3:13). To be human is to be able to describe and give some form of words to feelings and actions. Earlier in the Genesis story, Adam gives names to every living creature. Language development seems to be necessary for fully formed memories. When I was a youngster, I was fascinated with the story of Helen Keller and wondered about her life and awareness. Deaf, mute, and blind from early infancy, she did not learn her first words until she was seven. Later she described a wordless inner world as "an unconscious but conscious time of nothingness . . . a dark, silent imprisonment. I did not know . . . that I lived, acted or desired." Words are important to be able to remember or image the past and to imagine the future. With language grows an awareness of self as an individual and actor in relationship with others. One can empathetically see the lights going up in Helen Keller's private inner theater, as happens each morning in our own.

Language; a sense of past, present, and future; and a sense of the self as actor all seem to happen together. And they come together with story. Life is given a narrative shape to connect events and responses. Story is used to relate, to explain, to excuse: *The serpent tricked me*, or *This is why I was late to the meeting*.

How and why can humans do this? That which we experience comes through the five senses and happens in our minds. What is the relationship of interior mental experiences to the world we perceive? Is the world somehow story shaped with a narrative structure that is inherent in time and events? Or is it that our minds are so shaped as to give a story form to life? However we try to understand the relationship, we become aware that what we call *life* seems to be the result of a complex and often cryptic interplay between the world outside us and our efforts at interpretation, often through story. The very telling of a story seems to be based on a belief or some manner of hope that life either has or can be given significance and meaning.

We live, moreover, in a fleeting present. I go for a walk with Sydney. In the distance we see two deer and come across a young couple with another dog. The dogs run off together, and I have to call Sydney back. The air is warm and still, the ground dusty and dry. When I try to tell someone else of this experience, or even as I "tell" it to myself while I am experiencing it, I leave out many things. From out of their own private theaters, other people, I am aware, could tell it differently. They might highlight something in my conversation with the couple or about the breeds of the dogs. They might even transpose certain events to give them a different significance. People from one culture might pay more attention to the overall context of the story (the scenery and time of day), while others would put more emphasis on the participants. One can hear people arguing: "That didn't happen like that." "Yes, it did." "No, it didn't. I was there" "Well, so was I." We may in the end regard some tellings, or stories, as more accurate than others, but we recognize they all have their *fictional* quality. In some measure we are shaping events as they happen to us. We are making life up as we go along.

Who Was I?

My walk with Sydney took place fairly recently. What about the trip to my dad's parents' with my sisters many years earlier? It was so hot in their house in southern Illinois in July that the unfinished rooms upstairs were too uncomfortable to sleep in until the air had cooled at least a bit. So we were allowed to stay up late, and I can see us in the gathering darkness eating watermelon on their front porch, spitting seeds over the railing. In my memory's eye, I remember so clearly the back of my grandfather's head and the way the screen on the screen door pouched out. The next day we crossed on what seemed a huge bridge over the Mississippi River and went to a Cardinals game in St. Louis.

One of the more interesting mysteries of self-awareness involves our relationship with our earlier selves. If I am not sure exactly how I relate to myself of yesterday (one may especially sense this discrepancy if a wonderful or traumatic experience has intervened), how much less sure am I about the self of ten, twenty, or thirty years ago? All of us have had the experience of looking back and wondering who we were. We see a picture of ourselves taken years ago and are tempted to say, "Who was that guy?" or "Could she ever have imagined what I would be like now?" Or we try to imagine what we will be like some years from now.

Once I found myself in a puzzling dialogue with self and memory. I had returned to England to visit in Birmingham, where twenty years earlier Barbara and I had gone to live and work. In that earlier time, I was in my late twenties. I had just become a father and soon would become a father again—twice over with twins. I was embarked on a teaching career and was trying to finish a book I was writing.

I would sometimes take my son Benjamin to a small pond behind our house on the grounds of the college. In the springtime we would look at the wriggling black tadpoles and see our faces in the pond. It was to the same pond that I went twenty years later and looked in. I saw my face and remembered and then imagined I was seeing myself from those years ago and was in some kind of communication. I looked away and then stared back. He seemed to want to ask me something about what had happened, and I wondered what he thought of me. I trailed back from the pond bemused and puzzled.

One may, I realized, look back on an earlier self and be critical of immaturity, of unwise decisions, or of missed opportunities. Or in the guise of an earlier self, one may be surprised at what a later self has become. We become aware of how much people do change and are changing. I am, in more ways than one, a different person than I was and will be. Indeed, one could well maintain that there is no one true identity for the self. The self is many selves—past and present—viewed from different perspectives. Even on one day, as we have different moods, do various tasks, and are in a variety of relationships, we may regard ourselves as rather different selves. I have *personalities* as a son, husband, father, neighbor, supervisor, colleague, and friend. Some days I particularly notice this as I change identities with clothes—from pajamas to a suit to shorts and a baseball cap, then back into pajamas. We are, in many ways, a collection of selves.

Yet one may also recognize how self-awareness can be aware of all this, providing a larger perspective and an awareness of the changing yet ongoing self, which includes the past, present, and future. It remembers and supplies for us a form of narrative identity about our lives—embodying plot, personal agency, and future accountability. Indeed, I am often in the process of revising stories of my life from the perspective of new experiences and insights as part and parcel of my account of selfhood. I have an awareness and identity that is aware of my many selves.

Pearlie Forgets

More problematic for our sense of selfhood is what happens when the brain is damaged or begins to deteriorate. Often it is when something goes wrong with the brain that we get our best insights into how it functions and realize how dependent mind is upon brain. Psychologists and others have done extensive studies with people who have had major brain traumas or parts of their brains cut out as a result of surgery to fix some larger problem. Sometimes there are losses of certain functions like smell or taste or aspects of memory. Some people's physical eyes will still function, yet they cannot see. Others may lose decision-making ability or the power to restrain or inhibit themselves, causing them to behave in bizarre ways. Sometimes other parts of the brain are able partially or fully to compensate, but not always.

When my mother was in her late eighties, this bright, active woman, who was still reading and playing a smart game of bridge, began telling us that she was feeling "flaky." She made a kind of joke of it, and I reminded her that we all are forgetful from time to time.

In a few more months we could see what she meant. She would walk to the store and forget why she went. Clerks would call and tell us she was wandering around aimlessly. In the neighborhood, somewhat to our horror, she began picking people's flowers, commenting on how pretty they were. In a way it was funny and childlike, but also sad. "What are we going to do now?" she asked frequently, her short-term memory slipping badly. Soon, although she could read, she couldn't remember what she had read, and books were no longer her pleasure.

Pearl was diagnosed as having Alzheimer's disease, but I never believed that. I realize that this can be a kind of general diagnosis, but Pearl did not show the deterioration or more severe personality changes that go with Alzheimer's. Although in some ways childlike and often bored because of her circumstances, she still had a pleasant and at times even cheery disposition. Her physical health was otherwise quite good for someone her age.

On the positive side, the hard wiring, as it were, of her long-term memory remained in reasonable shape. We were able to have good conversations about earlier days. Rather surprisingly, she still got my jokes. I thought at first she might be faking it (there was a certain coping slyness about her mental condition), but if the jokes were not too complicated (a longer story requiring memory), she laughed without prompting in the right places.

Recognizing this and her former love for card games, I tried an experiment. "Pearlie," I asked, "Do you remember how to play tic-tac-toe?" "Sure," she replied, although she would often say that. I drew the design for the nine spaces. "Do you want to be Xs or Os?" I asked. "Xs," she said and picked up the pencil. She won the fourth game.

From that we graduated to the rather simple card game of War. I then went down to the toy store and brought home the cards for Go Fish. Playing also with my sister, Pearl was soon collecting Olivia Octopuses and Sammy Seahorses.

The next day we tried Solitaire. Although she needed a bit of coaching, Pearlie began to put most of the cards in the right places. I could see her memory both straining and gaining a little and was amazed at the ways even the deteriorating brain can function. In another couple of years, however, the deterioration became more pronounced. She became further confused and, shortly before she died, had to struggle even to say my name.

Growing Awareness

For all of us, the story starts at the beginning. When Benjamin was first born, I had so little understanding of babies that I thought their minds were total blanks. I would, I imagined, need to teach him everything. I was not aware that he had in his head a little learning machine that, with only some help, could soon begin to scheme and figure out many things for himself.

At first, however, the infant is not reflective and in dialogue with the self. We do not criticize little Benjy or any baby for this, any more than we would criticize a dog or a cat for its self-centeredness. But as the child grows, we begin to have higher hopes and expectations for it because it is a human being. Even before the age of two, a child begins to become reflective of the consequences of its actions. It may puzzle over what happens when the toilet is flushed or, as our twins, Matthew and Stuart, did in one of their "experiments," why the bar of Ivory soap does not go down with the flush.

The little child may try to understand why the parent is so displeased when the milk is spilled. He or she begins to think of the self as an actor in interaction with others.

Our expectations of the child grow, perhaps too soon at times. We begin to ask the child to have some sense of what it feels like and what it means to hit another infant on the head with a wooden block. To understand this blow as more than something that displeases the parent or child-minder, the youngster must develop a form of empathy. There needs to be a capacity to imagine what being hit on the head would feel like to another.

There can then be at least the dawning of a version of the negative golden rule: "Do not do to others what you do not want done to yourself." This may begin only in self-interested terms (so they won't hit you back), but even to have some awareness of self-interest is the beginning of a developing self-awareness.

Despite our projections with regard to how sweet little children are, it may not be until a child is six or seven that there is enough development to bring about a true measure of conscience and legitimate expectations with regard to the consequences of actions. The growth may then continue as a lifelong process. If asked to describe a mature human being, many people would do so in words that, in one way or another, portray a developed self-awareness. A mature person is able to perceive the self in thought and action. She or he can see how one interacts with others and is able to be self-critical and responsible—responding in thoughtful ways.

But with self-awareness and an accompanying awareness of others come challenges. There is not only the negative version of the golden rule that tells us not to do to others what we do not want to happen to us. There is a more positive way of thinking and acting. There can develop not only a sense of the good one wants for oneself but also a sense of the common good—what is in all our interests.

By taking others into account, one also shows an awareness of their awareness—of their full humanity. This allows for genuine friendships and forms of community. In conversation and interaction, one becomes present to them. One makes something of one's own awareness available to them. As I become more aware of another's awareness and make myself more available, I become aware, too, of her awareness responding to mine and then of our shared awareness of this. So may we put ourselves in another's shoes and, as the saying goes, walk the walk with them. Life becomes richer and more deeply layered.

With such awareness one may also come to believe that at least a measure of self-transcendence and the potential for even reaching beyond self-interest exists. Thomas Aquinas once described human beings as rational animals capable of laughter. They can see their mixed motivations and the discrepancies, contradictions, and ironies of their lives. They develop the capacity to choose and make choices based on enlightened self-interest and a common good. Perhaps we may be willing to go further and act for the good of others, even when it requires giving up something of benefit to the self. One may accomplish all sorts of things in life, but becoming a person with such a developed awareness and capability, I have come to believe, would surely be life's greatest adventure.

But Can One Choose?

From various philosophical, psychological, and biological perspectives, however, the concept of going beyond self-centered motivations to act for the good of others has been seen as illusionary. Humans may imagine they might do this. They may think they are choosing certain thoughts and actions freely, but in reality, it is argued, they are not and cannot. Because of the ways our minds as well as our bodies have developed through a long evolutionary process, functions and limitations directed by brain structures and deep psychic forces control all human actions. Although it may not be possible to predict every human action, it is possible, on the basis of these understandings, to explain them afterward. We can study the activities of other species and see that their actions, though they may appear to be freely chosen and sometimes taken for reasons that appear altruistic, are actually directed by basic instincts for self- or species-preservation. So, it is argued, this is finally true of human beings as well. All that is needed to identify this determinism is enough information. The mother bird drags her wing as though she is wounded and calls the predator's attention to herself; this may cost her life, but it preserves the lives of her chicks. The dominant male baboon puts himself on exposed sentry duty for the protection of his offspring, nephews, and nieces. He is driven to do this by instincts, deep within, that help his particular clan and genetic pool to persevere. Every human activity, some contend, can be explained as a response (admittedly a more complex one than is found in other animals) to forms of such programming of the brain and mind. From one sociobiological perspective, individual persons are, in the last analysis, essentially containers for the genetic material that is blindly striving for its continuation.

I decide to stop the car and help a person with a flat tire. I do this even though it will delay me and I could be exposing myself to some danger. If you knew enough about the hundreds of generations of evolutionary selection and programming that have formed me, and if you knew about my parents and how I was brought up as a middle child, the fact that I don't like living with a troubled conscience, and so forth, you would be able to predict that I would stop. Or, if I had young kids with me in the car, you would be able to predict that I would not stop.

You go to help out in a soup kitchen for homeless people—same thing!—perhaps with some imbedded need to help preserve the species. The sociobiologist argues that morality, or more strictly the human belief in morality, is an adaptation that furthers reproductive ends. Ethics are regarded as a shared illusion of the human race. The illusion of altruism has developed as a strategy or game with the object of getting others to cooperate. But it *is* a game: if others will never reciprocate, my offer will have to be withdrawn. I will give you some of my food, but if I run short and you never give anything in return, sooner more likely than later, the game will have to end. I may say that I will live and play fairly, not only if you will live fairly but so you can live fairly, too. But if you insist on living unfairly, I will try only so many times to get you to go along.

Indeed, the last century and a half of behavioral study and discovery can be seen to have tightened the strictures around any idea of human freedom, moral or otherwise. Evolutionary, physiological, psychological, cultural, and genetic insights have been used to maintain that all human activities are determined. However much humans may imagine or want their lives to be special, and granting the complexities and richness of their cultures, their lives are still controlled by the same forces for preservation and survival that govern the lives of other animals. Although the majority of people may not be able to give names to these theories, they have penetrated deeply into the contemporary psyche. They contribute to a sense of relativism and the ennui of the postmodern self: *What difference does it make? I really don't have that much choice.* In some ways these feelings of determination have taken the place of the old one-size-fits-all excuse "The devil made me do it."

Fractional Freedom

One can, however, recognize the power of deterministic understandings while still believing they do not tell the whole story. With the development of thinking on thinking, of reflectiveness, self-awareness, and self-criticism, have come organizations and hierarchies of thought that are influential from the top down. Rather than being heavily programmed for only certain kinds of learning, the human brain/mind, with its inductive, deductive, and other powers, is remarkably flexible. It has learned to adapt functions that were formed, for instance, for hunting, to scan the sky for tomorrow's weather, and to take on other purposes, such as algebra and poetry. That openness, in large part, makes the brain capable of all manner of creativity. Human actions become more complex than just the result of forces working upward, as it were, from genetic programming, brain chemistry, and deep psychic energy. Moreover, the many things humans think and do have now become a highly social as well as an individual phenomenon that needs to be set in the context of culture with the transmission of information and understanding. We are the only beings that carry on culture in any significant way. This context involves memory, language, and institutions, along with the passing on of not just genes but also tradition and education. If one imagines a kind of science-fiction time when humans would pass along their culture to aliens from another galaxy or to highly developed computers, this transmission of knowledge and understandings—apart from genes—would be more evident. In this light such transmissions can be seen taking place when different cultures encounter one another.

Genetic, brain-structural, psychological, and also cultural-deterministic forces are still very strong. Evolutionary psychology, as an extension of evolutionary biology, certainly helps in the understanding of how the brain/mind developed. The difference that self-awareness brings may well be but a small part of human life, affecting only a fraction of thought and behavior. This remarkable ability to be aware of ourselves and reflect on ourselves in our thinking and action can, however, be seen as the leverage that makes an enormous difference in our appreciation of the potential of being human. In dynamic systems, we now know, little perturbations can have great consequences. In the familiar analogy, the flutter of a butterfly's wings in China may change the weather in Seattle. Similarly, the fractional capacity for choice in human life, together with the development of a larger sense of self that can make choices on behalf of others as well as from self-interest, introduces a new range of possibilities and opportunities. Even if one decides to regard this capacity as only an enlarged form of self-interest, the empathetic inclusion of others and the willingness, as it were, to make room for them, enable a maturity that helps to make for the fullness of humanity. It is a kind of leverage in the hierarchies of the mind that influences the parts and keeps one from being simply controlled by or reduced to them.

I think, for instance, of my sons Matthew and Stuart, identical twins, who have the same genetic material and were brought up in the same family and community. Yet how different they now are. Indeed, as they grew one could see them striving to develop distinguishing characteristics. One could even imagine two cloned babies raised in highly similar circumstances but with myriad possibilities offered by the slightest of brain differences and early developmental experiences. These would then cascade as the brain developed, and, along with life's complexity and their ability to exercise awareness and its fractional leverage, would surely enable them to become dissimilar in numerous ways.

Human beings obviously do not exercise their potential for awareness and some measure of freedom over their lives with any great consistency. Such developed awareness of and greater perspective on self may be seen as both a partially known goal *and* an achievement in most if not all lives. But the capacity to see oneself in perspective, to take others into account, and to lessen or in some measure transcend ego gives meaning to the biblical injunction "to lose one's life in order to find it." In the lessening of the self-centered ego, one may discover a larger self that includes ego and may be said in some measure to begin to transform it. It is a quality that also enables one to be genuinely present to others— to be a presence and more than a self-striving, surviving ego. It is a capacity that enables one to wonder about whether and how human life might be said to have significance in the universe.

Two ⚭ In a Real World

Dance and Dancer

As one drives southwest from the busy city of London and through its suburbs and outlying towns, there on the Salisbury Plain—out of our time and civilizations—stand the mysterious megaliths of Stonehenge. I remember going there as a young man, when one was allowed to wander about more freely and touch the massive stones. They were erected several thousand years ago by a people about whom we know little. We can still only guess at how they managed to move and raise the great stones there. Carefully aligned to the movement of the sun, moon, and stars, Stonehenge was evidently an attempt to decipher the mysteries of the sky and seasons. Perhaps it was a way of worship as well.

Conscious and aware human beings are a marvel, and so is the world in which they live. Reflective humans have found many ways to wonder about their place in this world. From earliest times they pondered the patterns and intricacies of life and death and new life. Knowing creation to be spectacular, they trembled in awe at lightning's bolt and thunder's crunch. They lifted their eyes to the star-thronged skies. "O look at all the fire-folk sitting in the air! The bright boroughs, the circle citadels there," exclaimed Gerard Manley Hopkins. They marveled at the movement of the stars and planets, the haunting moonrise in all its phases, and the sun's majestic setting and return. One can imagine our ancestors' wonder and hear their praise in hymns and songs. "The heavens are telling the glory of God, / and the firmament proclaims [God's] handiwork" (Psalm 19:1). And here are we with our consciousness and awareness to behold it: must not someone or something have made all this?

As our ancestors bowed themselves in reverence and gratitude, it was often hard not to worship the creation itself along with the One they believed to be the Creator. How distinguishable are they? "How can we know the dancer from the dance?" asked the poet William Butler Yeats.

Some years after my visit to Stonehenge, I traveled to the high Andes of Peru. I awoke early one morning to watch the sunrise over the ruins of the Incan temple, terraced gardens, and citadel at Machu Picchu. I found myself praying what became a poem:

> I am up this morning as your sun rises,
>> the return incredible again,
> burgundy warming to gold on horizon's hearth.
> I imagine other spectacles through myriad ages,
>> in different shapes, colors and speeds,
>> on countless worlds of cold and fiery beauty;
>> and I am out of mind.
> Birds herald and call me happily back.
> Their trees grow green, each its own shrine.
> Crowned, you burst forth, emblazoning the sky
> before and beyond, reflecting all things.
> And, though I think I know its dangers,
> I recognize my mothers and fathers come to worship you,
> for, bathed in light, I, too, am on my knees
> and see beyond all times and worlds
>> your shining here.

In All Directions

Yet within the last one hundred years—even within just the last two decades—how much more we know and how much less we know. When I returned to my alma mater to teach and preside over the vast gothic chapel at Princeton, our home was across the street from the astrophysics department. I was as fascinated by what was going on in Peyton Hall (and in my conversations with physicists and biologists) as I was by life in the chapel. The higher our knowledge climbs, the more we see to wonder over. New visual and X-ray telescopes mounted on satellites peer beyond all previous sight and back through the ages to the edges of the universe. Even our awe is overwhelmed. There are more than a hundred billion galaxies and uncounted, unimaginable stars, trillions of them, along with myriad quasars and black holes. A microscopic intricacy and simplicity exist that are equally wondrous and breathtaking. Not only are there the vast reaches of interstellar space, but a typical atom, if its nucleus were the size of a golf ball, would have its outermost electrons circling two miles away. As early as 1896, German physicist Emil Wiechert spoke of a universe "infinite in all directions, not only above us in the large but also below us in the small. If we start from the human scale of existence and explore the content of the universe further and further, we finally arrive, both in the large and in the small, at misty distances where first our senses and then our concepts fail us."

At every level scientists are astounded at the exact combinations and precise balancing of the forces that shape the universe. Gravity, the speed of cosmic expanse (both in the first rapid inflation and now in whatever is driving it afterward), the huge amounts of still-unaccounted-for dark matter and dark energy in the universe, whatever it is that gives mass to the universe, the weak and strong nuclear forces, the ratio of electron to proton mass, and the atomic structures of hydrogen and helium and the rest of the periodic table—all the physics and chemistry have to be just right for this kind of universe to exist and to allow life to come into being. The dials, as it were, are very finely tuned.

People continue to wonder whether this means there is a design behind and within it all. The astronomer Fred Hoyle, impressed by so many exacting "accidents," concluded that the universe looks like a "put-up job." The analogy of a crossword puzzle has been used, with all the right words carefully linked with one another. It would, however, need to be a crossword puzzle going in at least three or four dimensions.

Or is it all, in fact, some universal accident? Perhaps all we can surmise is that this is just the way things are for us to be here asking the questions. Maybe, as some have speculated, a multitude of universes are continuously popping out of black holes or vacuum fluctuations. This is ours. Sooner or later a universe came about with things arranged just right for carbon-based life.

In this universe, moreover, the timing had to be well nigh perfect for the forces to be able to fashion the first stars in which formed the heavier elements that are among the building blocks necessary for the intricate chemistry of life. In the stellar cataclysms of the dying and exploding of those stars, the atoms were blown back into space, later to become components of our solar system and our planet.

Then, too, the conditions were just right for there to be a planet Earth capable of bearing life. The size of our sun, the size of this Earth and its distance from the sun (not too close, not too far), the right amounts of atmosphere and ultraviolet radiation, having a great Jupiter in the right place to clear off many (but not all) of the asteroids and to deflect comets, all the chemical mixtures and balance here, quite possibly having a moon at the right distance, the right amount of time—all and more were necessary conditions.

And then the alchemy of life began. Life may exist in other conditions, but very specific forms of life developed here. Over several billion years, the process has led from the formation of the first cells to multicellular life and more and more complex forms. From the simplest genes, and then on the twined spirals of DNA, genetic codes developed. Through mating and sexual reproduction, genes, in multileveled interaction with the environment and other species, were able to keep on experimenting and testing. As the changes and genetic information were passed on over many more eons, consciousness and then its awareness came to life. The human genome, we now are coming to understand, is both simpler and more complex than previously imagined. Relatively fewer genes are essential for fashioning a human being, but the genome also contains a whole history of other genetic material, some from viruses and bacteria, that has been and is necessary in its own way for the evolutionary process.

Are We Accompanied?

Again one asks about any design or intent. Has there been a luring of thought to life? Are any characteristics of rationality—what the Greeks call *logos* (from which comes our word *logical*)—fundamental to existence? With that possibility in mind, I put together a poem I called "Bits":

> On waves in rippled space
> spirit broods, spreading
> the stellar ash transformed
> bursts into living
> dazzled knots in the flow,
> genetic wording
> to spiraled paragraphs,
> logos informing.
> From those light years away,
> whirlwinding and code,
> suffering awareness
> creation unfolds,
> a semiotic world,
> yet being told.

From the beginning of human existence, these thoughts and questions have been put in one form or another. Are our thinking and storytelling related to an important and even essential aspect of the universe? Are they of any significance? Or are they alone? Is our awareness, we now ask, but one of the phenomena of mindless evolutionary processes that will exist for a comparatively brief duration on an infinitesimally small part of a universe otherwise dark to the light of awareness?

There are, of course, billions of other galaxies and trillions of stars, and, one can imagine, millions of planets, with at least thousands of them capable of bearing life. From the example of this planet, one sees how, once life gets started, there seems to be a strong impetus toward more complexity and astounding diversity. Why not hundreds if not thousands of planets in various eons capable of developing sentient life? Many people want to believe this—even that we have been visited from other parts of the universe. Yet, maybe the conditions and timing for intelligent life to arise (life, for example, capable of the subjunctive and doing mathematics) are statistically more stringent than even millions of planets would allow for. And then, one realizes, despite billions of species now extinct and the millions now existing on Earth, only one species has finally come to awareness such as ours. And that took several billion years of continually right conditions. Despite the guesswork and the hopes of science-fiction writers, speculative scientists, and others, it is possible that the "glorious accident" of thinking on thinking and awareness has happened only once.

We do not know. Our human race may never know. In a universe whose galaxies seem to continue to flee apart as space expands, it is possible that no awareness exists other than this brief and limited one of ours. It may be a very strange and lonely phenomenon.

Do we sometimes feel otherwise only because we are afraid not to? Or, again, is awareness in some way essential to being?

Patterns and Accidents

As we further seek to understand the characteristics of life, we also now recognize that there are many forms of reality that are not carefully ordered. Dripping taps, turbulent fluids, clouds, fibrillating hearts, and many of the brain's activities are examples of processes in which behavior appears to be highly random and genuinely chaotic. That is true of a number of subatomic processes as well. At the same time there is an ongoing interplay between the chaotic and the ordering principles and patterns that bring shape to our universe. Regularity and irregularity are both necessary. Without a fine balance between stability and instability, life as we know it could not be. There would be either total chaos or a frozen stasis. Chance and patterning, chaos and self-organizing processes, possibility and strong probability, play and propensities, are all part of the dance—a dialogue of life that has long intrigued many a musician, poet, and painter.

From out of the flux, forms emerge. Perhaps a few simple templates guide all manner of patterning processes at deep generative levels, as programs encoded in basic algorithms are constantly repeated in the midst of randomness. Randomness continues to produce novelty. And gesturing within the dance seems to be some ratchet or uptick favoring complexity in an evolutionary current that can be brutal as well as beautiful, terrifying, tragic, and awesome.

More and more we are coming to understand that at the fundamentals of existence, this sort of interplay is going on. Deep in subatomic levels, where activity, according to our efforts to measure and describe, has characteristics of both particles and waves, there exists not what we might think of as substance, but relationships—energy emerging from the intersecting fields of space-time in knots or kinks that develop patterns. The energy is always changing. It is the forms and patterns that continue, even while they express probabilities about what can be rather than following rigid rules. The physicist John Wheeler, who sometimes verges on the poetic to describe what he finds happening, speaks of "events so numerous and uncoordinated that, flaunting freedom from formula, they yet fabricate firm form."

Quantum Queerness and Connections

The principles of quantum mechanics, now central to efforts to interpret what is happening at the subatomic stratum of existence, present a number of understandings that seem counterintuitive. Where energy radiates or is absorbed not continuously but discontinuously in quanta or little indivisible units, there would seem to be circumstances of uncertainty that can be resolved only when some form of observation takes place. For example, the direction, or spin, of one of a pair of particles separated from each other seems to be determined only when the other is determined. Until then its spin is not only unknown, it cannot be said to exist. The observed spin of one of the pair seems to determine that of the other, even when the distance over which they would need to communicate is greater than could be traversed at the speed of light—the apparent cosmic speed limit. They remain connected in some manner of quantum "entanglement." Albert Einstein (to whom I, as a young undergraduate, once waved a greeting on the sidewalks of Princeton) spoke of such communication as "spooky action at a distance." John Wheeler repeats the theme: "The act of observation creates a real situation in which otherwise there would only be ghostly uncertainty."

What is happening? Or in what manner of context is this happening such that observation causes the particles to be chosen for their part in the dance? They seem to pass through some way of being observed or some sieve of existence that gives them definition and lets them be from indeterminacy. The ghostly mists of possibilities and the fuzziness of the subatomic world then solidify into what we know as life.

Some physicists have suggested that such surprising features of quantum mechanics may result from a time when the universe was much smaller. It is a kind of memory of an era when there may have been as many as ten dimensions—nine of them dimensions of space and the tenth, a dimension of time. Perhaps, it is also imagined, there may be still another dimension of time—or something like what we call "time since time," and its relations to the other dimensions are still far from understood. Four of those dimensions developed as the space-time that we experience, while the others that never developed remain minuscule and sort of enfolded in each other. Still, however, a deeper interconnectedness of the universe could be happening through the enfolded levels where space and time do not count in the same way they do in the four-dimensional world. Or, others have suggested, there may be a way of understanding the dimensions to be folding and unfolding in ongoing fluctuations in a labyrinthine universe. Such a theory could help explain some of the apparent oddities of quantum reality such as the principle of indeterminacy, the wave/particle duality, and other both/and features in a world where protons can be both "round" and "nonround." In any case, the many linkages and cross-influences in a universe that now seems far more like an organism than a machine might begin to find partial explanation in some form of this implication. "All things . . . linked are, that thou canst not stir a flower / Without troubling a star," wrote Francis Thompson, anticipating our inklings regarding the intricate interlocking of physics, biology, and now thought within the universal ecosystem.

Aspects of the folding or curving up in these other dimensions could be regarded as the tiny (myriad times smaller than atoms) curvatures that some scientists imagine to be at the core of all electrons and quarks. They may be imagined to be the *strings* that some physicists postulate to be the incredibly minute vibrations at the heart of subatomic existence. One thinks of the whole subatomic world quivering. These strings could also be imagined to be the notes of the music of the dance of the universe.

A Shining Through

Quantum physics works. It is a powerful explanatory methodology. But how it works is still much of a mystery even to its best practitioners. Some are content to leave it at that—as just the interesting and strange ways things are. Others speculate further about the intimate interconnectedness of all life, along with the realization that some manner of observation or awareness may be fundamental to being and existence. The notes of the strings could be viewed as functions of mathematics and *logos*. The memory and connectedness, along with the fundamental observation, might be regarded as characteristics of profound reflection. Because we now know that many physical systems, even some very simple ones, carry information and have the capacity to compute, it has been suggested that the countless atomic processes going on all the time could even be regarded as a gigantic cosmic computation.

Poets turn to the image of light to suggest some manner of observation or making observable—a being seen, a letting be seen, a letting be. They tell of a significance that shines through all things. Much of Hopkins's poetry issued from his intuition of the "inscape" and "instress" of all life. "It will flame out, like shining from shook foil." The essayist and critic George Steiner also glimpses "a shining through." In many religions God's creativity and presence to the world are intuited in terms of light that is itself invisible and silent. Near the beginning of the Gospel of John, we read that "all that comes to be is alive with the life of *logos*" and that this life is light for all. Indeed, the Bible's story of creation begins, in Hopkins's words, as "the Holy Ghost over the bent / World broods with warm breast and with ah! bright wings." Then God says, "Let there be light."

Steiner more often refers to sound, which he imagines to be akin to the background radiation of creation, and which we might also associate with the vibrations of the minute subatomic strings. This is heard, Steiner suggests, in "poetry, art and music that relate us most directly to that in being which is not ours." "Music, above all, is the unwritten theology." When I think of music in this way and rejoice in all the singing and symphony we may do together, I hear Bach or, before him, Vivaldi— the plain chords, the repetition with the tricks and surprises, the harmonic adventures, the interplay of chance and symmetry, the dance.

Some scientists are more explicit with their intuitions or beliefs. Perhaps observation—an awareness necessary to being—is necessary only at the quantum level of uncertainty and not at the level of otherwise predictable events. Yet, because in dynamic systems all is interconnected, might this awareness still be seen as fundamental for being? Might it be the context for existence? "The idea of a universal Mind or logos would be, I think, a fairly plausible inference from the present state of scientific theory; at least it is in harmony with it," reasoned the renowned physicist Erwin Schrödinger. "The universe," suggested Sir James Jeans, "gradually begins to look more like a great thought than a great machine." "[C]onscious awareness of the world," maintains the mathematical physicist Paul Davies, "is not a meaningless and incidental quirk of nature, but an absolutely fundamental facet of reality."

Other scientists, of course, would not attempt to interpret the evidence in that way. Or, at least as scientists, they would say they do not know. Some would even reject the "ghostly" language of Einstein and Wheeler as too much like mysticism. Talk of a universal Mind is not only unnecessary for these scientists, it could get in the way of an aesthetic logic that is on the way to explaining the universe without any such referent. Several of the more recent cosmological guesses attempt to avoid the conundrum of infinite regress, that is, if something was there for a universe to be made of, what was before that for that to be made of? And on and on. If one postulates God, what made God? It has been suggested that the "big bang," from which it is believed came at once space, time, and matter, and then all creation, happened from some fluctuation in nothingness. All existence, which comes from this "bubble," then inflated at a fantastic rate. Echoing the theological idea of *creatio ex nihilo* (that God created from nothing), these scientists hold that everything comes from nothing, but, in a way, that nothing more is needed to explain it. In attempting to explain why there is not nothing (or why there is more than nothing), such theories of beginnings, like the first chapters of Genesis and the creation myths of other religions, provide an alternative story of the universe. A universe of continuous creation—a universe that was always here and without beginning, by way of contrast, could have no such story.

Nothing, however, is itself turning into a tricky scientific subject. As philosophers and mathematicians have known for a long time, once nothing is given a name, it becomes something. The number zero has all manner of influences and functions, as does the *off* in binary computations and computer chips. Holes in a donut or a piece of clothing are full of significance. The different spaces between the particles of an atom are teeming with implications and active with force fields, as is the space between Earth and the sun. Empty space, some scientists suggest, might be compared to a blank paper full of creases and ripples that would influence anything that comes into contact with it.

But, one might say, many of these examples of empty space and nothingness come from circumstances and conditions that already exist. What of the nothingness before there was anything? But, again, nothing-ness, once named, has become a kind of thing—an empty something of potentiality, perhaps in some way related to the dark energy that some now believe to be a vital part of the missing something of the universe. Nothing might, then, be thought of as a vast storehouse of opportunities waiting to appear—a perfect symmetry ready for the slightest imbalancing to make something out of nothing. Again there is an echo of the idea of God creating out of the potentialities of the divine imagination. In turn, God could be imagined as the nothingness from which creation emerges, for still, almost hidden within these secular hypotheses of something from nothing, there seems to be some form of presupposition that allows for the oxymoron there *is* nothing—that nothing is. There still seems to be at least potential for grammar and mathematics—a context of equations in which there could be fluctuations. From those arguing that there need be nothing for creation to be, there seems to be some premise of *logos* that precedes or transcends the existing universe. This premise seems essential, even while proponents of the universe out of nothing contend that the physical and mathematical worlds would have had to come into being together, while the *time* of space-time might be regarded as a human construct or interpretation.

The bottom line, however, is that all of us are beyond our understanding. I certainly am. No one is able to prove by means of scientific study the existence of a universal Mind or Awareness to which human awareness might be related. Fifty years into the future, the evidence may look rather different, with yet other mysteries to delve into. Even if it seemed that the evidence now gestured in the direction of the existence of Awareness, we would still be a long way from understanding the *character* of this fundamental quality or context of existence—whether, for instance, we could regard it as intentional. Then there would be questions as to whether, by our understanding, we could find such a God to be interested in the creation and be well-intentioned toward human awarenesses. Would God want to be in relationship with us? Any such beliefs would need to be explored in other dimensions of human experience along with the scientific. We would need to reflect on other kinds of stories and ways of thinking about life.

What We Would See

We again need to acknowledge that still many questions remain about all forms of human experiencing and knowing. Recall the time when I was out walking with my dog and met another couple and their dog. One thinks of all the ways that incident might be experienced, told, and remembered. We are always interpreting, and, as we wonder about what we may be reasonably sure about, we find ourselves asking at once questions of physiology, physics, psychology, and philosophy. Given our amazing mental capacities and the rapid expansion of learning, we yet remain limited amid the vastness and minuteness of creation. We are stuck in the middle, as it were, and limited to the five senses and their restrictions with respect to all that is above and below their reach. We are also limited by the restrictions of the technology and the mathematics and logic we use to try to enhance our study of what is otherwise beyond us. We have, as well, no direct experience of any other dimensions. Then we have only our brains' ways of interpreting all the bits—the dots and dashes—that come through our senses. We do not and cannot appropriate a reality outside us. We can only try to interpret it.

As a young student, I remember being intrigued by a mental picture drawn, Plato tells us, by Socrates. Human beings, whether educated or not, are chained up in a subterranean cavern. They are unable to see anything but occasional shadows cast on a wall by figures passing in front of a fire above them. Out beyond there was a *real* world, but they could not know this world directly from inside their cave. To our contemporary way of thinking, Plato's image may remind us that our experience of life happens only within our ways of understanding. With all our skills and daring, we cannot get outside ourselves. Rather than seeing things as they are, we see things as we are. The poet Wallace Stevens intended a similar thought when he observed that we do not live in a place, "we live in the description of a place." The Mississippi River, Mark Twain noted, could look quite different when he saw her as a writer or as a riverboat pilot. In many ways we decide what kind of a "place" we will live in as we see not only what we are able to see but what we are prepared to see and want to see and then try to give it description. Einstein, who remained bothered by the seeming unsettling randomness at the heart of the universe, held that God (as he understood God) would not play dice with the universe. He could not accept the principle of indeterminacy, which holds that certain aspects of the sub-atomic world are inherently unpredictable. And, he could not see what he could not accept.

When I was a child, I liked to stare at those drawings that would first seem one thing and then another. In one of them, two dark faces are seen in profile. It can take some time to recognize that one could also concentrate on the *empty* section and come to see a white vase. For a time afterward, it may be hard to see the faces again. And why did I see the faces rather than the vase in the first place? More disquieting is a Rorschach test, in which one may project any number of interpretations onto an ambiguous inkblot design. Now, in the field of literary criticism, some interpreters hold that a text can be read any number of ways and have any number of meanings—none necessarily more privileged or "true" than another. Some of the same multiplicities are applicable to the sciences and every human endeavor. There are those who suggest that contemporary physics, the concept of time, and even the elegance and apparent truths of mathematics, on which all science depends, are not discoveries of what is really *there*—inherent in reality—but constructs and projections of the human mind looking for patterns and rationality.

Insiders

In one of the most difficult passages of the Bible, Jesus—the teller of parables—says to his disciples, "To you has been given the secret of the kingdom of God, but for those outside, everything comes in parables; in order that / 'they may indeed look, but not perceive, / and may indeed listen, but not understand'" (Mark 4:11–12). The words are challenging because we think the understanding of the parables should be available to all hearers. Why else did Jesus teach? Indeed, a number of interpreters believe that later bearers of the tradition put the present form of these words in Jesus' mouth. Must hearers be on the inside—in some sense already having committed themselves—before the parables can help them discern the secret of God's kingdom—God's ways in the world? It seems unfair. Yet, just as the scientist may need to adopt a hypothesis before he or she can see if it works, so there may be ways in which some form of commitment is required of all life's discoveries. I realize that I cannot just sit outside and observe. Each of us must participate in order to know.

A novice Buddhist monk was once crossing over a bridge with his master when he made the mistake of asking how deep the river below was. Only after a fierce struggle did he keep himself from being thrown into the water. Perhaps he could have been told "twelve feet," but the only way of really *knowing* the depth of the cold, rushing river was to plunge in.

We may drive by the woods looking at the trees and undergrowth through the car window. Or we may stop and hike into the woods for a very different experience. Both the hiker and the woods will in some measure be changed by that participation.

We all are part of the world we are trying to understand. Our world of experience is not something without us that we can dispassionately examine. It is a world we are within and that is within us. In and with this world we must interact. We are in many ways ourselves dancers within all the dancing. We must make choices as to how we will dance, and our choices will shape and have an effect on what we experience.

The Underwriting

It may seem, then, that there are as many different woods and rivers as those who walk or swim in them. There is, of course, truth in this understanding, and we cannot know for sure what is in another person's private theater—whether, for instance, someone else sees red as I do. A text, too, has as many meanings as it has readers. But is all then wholly relative? Is every interpretation of the same value? Certitude, however much some may claim it, seems beyond human grasp, but still there is the quest for understanding. Can the sciences not at least approximate forms of reality? Do not the statistical propensities that we find in the natural world at least resemble some laws of nature regarding what truly is and must be? Is there not a crucial concordance between the *laws* of physics and the mathematical functions that *describe* those laws—a link between mathematics and reality? In the social and moral realms, are there as many holocausts as there are interpreters of it? Was and is slavery wrong only for those who think it is wrong at a given time? Is there no basis for shared understanding? The modern and postmodern world continues to press these questions first posed in some of their extreme forms by the Dada (meaningless babble) movement of artists, and since taken on (fittingly sometimes in their own kind of well-refined babble) by the deconstructionist theorists.

In his book *Real Presences*, George Steiner searches for this basis—some thing or One, if you will, with whom we may dance: "[A]ny coherent understanding of what language is and how language performs, . . . any coherent account of human speech to communicate meaning and feeling is, in the final analysis, underwritten by the assumption of God's presence." Every experience will be known individually, but there is that which underwrites our communication. It is, maintains Steiner, the wager of every artist that the "sayability" of existence—the ability to express and communicate something about life—is underwritten by a form of presence and *logos*. Deep down ("deep down things," as Hopkins would have it), one reckons, is a covenant or link between description and object that makes possible a cosmos—a world of music and poetry and stories. The sculptor Henry Moore agreed in the sense that if by religion one means that life has some significance, "art in itself is akin to religion, . . . in fact, another expression of the belief that life is worth living."

There is as well, one wants to believe, a significance and reality inherent in the art of mathematics—the logic that seems the necessary context for all being. For some this faith may even be described as a value judgment based in the beauty of mathematical forms and the science dependent on them. "Rigorous argument," confesses the mathematical physicist Roger Penrose, "is usually the *last* step! Before that one has to make many guesses, and for these, aesthetic convictions are enormously important."

If there is this underwriting, how might it be appreciated? If there is some ultimate rationality or *logos*, some ground for significance—some Spirit of being and life—can there be for us any manner of relationship?

Three ❧ In Spirit and Spirit

Go-Between God

A number of scientists seem to view the world and its constituent parts strictly from the past and from below. From the subatomic universe have "bubbled up" more complex forms, including finally life and consciousness, but these are to be explained only as the coming together of their parts. Their linkage and the appearance of mind and awareness are interesting phenomena but are not to be viewed as resulting from any organizing principles or direction in the universe. Underneath all that exists is lifelessness, from which life comes and to which it returns. Everything that is could be based in a few simple constituents that science might be close to discovering.

Other scientists and thinkers, however, are impressed by the ways things do link together and seem to be responding to inherent possibilities. Some might not go so far as to give a status to this inherent *eros*, this love of coming together, to organize, take shape, and create genetic and other forms of information. They might not have a name for the tendency to develop maximum diversity and greater complexity, but they do observe something else besides what can be explained only in terms of the parts. They would agree, moreover, that to say that the parts just tend to organize themselves is really no explanation.

In his book *The Go-Between God*, John Taylor imagines the Spirit of God to be at the heart of all interrelating. This Spirit of life allows for the connections of a universe that can be comprehended. The Spirit's observing enables cause and effect and the links between mind and mathematics, making science possible. It is Hopkins's "instress." It provides for what one hymn calls "the mystic harmony linking sense to sound and sight." This Spirit lets present, past, and future be in relationship, and so offers opportunity for language and narrative. It enables and encourages human awareness with awareness of others, and so sympathy, communication, and community. It is that potential for creation's sayability—that *Logos* or Word that speaks out of the silence and allows the world to be seen and described. It is the underwriting of a life of music, poetry, and stories.

God's Awareness

But how would human beings know or relate to this Spirit? How would one have any relationship?

Three approaches are sometimes used to try to think about some human apprehension of divine Spirit. The first may be called realism, or sometimes naïve realism. This view regards the reality of God as actually appearing in human life and at times even speaking human and recordable words. When, for instance, the Apostle Paul is deeply troubled because of what he describes as his "thorn . . . in the flesh" and hears a voice that tells him, "My grace is sufficient for you, for power is made perfect in weakness" (2 Corinthians 12:7,9), the realist regards these words as coming from outside Paul and being heard through his physical ears. A nonrealist's understanding goes the other direction. Nothing is happening outside Paul's mind. What he hears is a result of the emotional and spiritual struggle he is undergoing. This he projects onto an imagined exterior reality.

A third perspective, called critical realism, would not deny that Paul may have had an encounter with a reality that is beyond him, but it also happens in his mind and takes the particular form it does because of Paul's own life and experience. Paul himself may have given us a way of thinking about such a relationship when he used a kind of analogy for the Spirit of God being something like the human spirit:

> The Spirit searches everything, even the depths of God. For what human being knows what is truly human except the human spirit that is within? So also no one comprehends what is truly God's except the Spirit of God. (1 Corinthians 2:10–11)

The human spirit to which Paul refers sounds like what one could also call our self-awareness—the way we can be conscious about thinking and reflecting on ourselves. God's Spirit, Paul intimates, is like a divine Awareness. Now, knowing something of the dimensions of the universe, we would, of course, have to imagine some immense awareness to be the Awareness of the God of all that exists. But, as I have thought about the analogy, I realized how it might encourage an insight into the experience of awareness with Awareness—of the human spirit with the divine.

One can notice how many men and women of prayer seem to speak of or allude to a form of this relationship. They do so from a variety of backgrounds and traditions. Often they use the language of searching and journeying inward. In gaining a deeper or greater awareness of self, there may come a sense of greater Awareness.

In the twelfth century, a Christian teacher known as Richard of St. Victor advised, "If you wish to search out the deep things of God, search out first of all the depth of your own spirit." Two centuries later the anonymous author of *The Cloud of Unknowing* offered this counsel: "Strain every nerve in every possible way to know and experience yourself as you truly are. It will not be long, I suspect, before you have a real knowledge and experience of God as God is." Through one's awareness and experience of oneself, a person may come, these writers suggest, to a relationship with the divine Awareness of life.

In the twentieth century, the Orthodox theologian Anthony Bloom intimated that we need to journey through ourselves "in order to emerge at the deepest level of self in to the place where God is, the point at which

God and I meet." Similarly Thomas Merton held, "The fact is . . . that if you descend into the depths of your own spirit . . . and arrive somewhere near the center of where you *are*, you are confronted with the inescapable truth that at the very root of your existence you are in constant and immediate and inescapable contact with the infinite power of God."

The theologian Paul Tillich described the experience in terms of coming to know the self as the presence of God is realized. He wrote of discovering ourselves when we discover God. "Man discovers something identical with himself though it transcends him infinitely—something from which he is estranged, but from which he never has been and never will be separated."

With and Without Us

The daring and intimacy of the language are remarkable. The relationship may seem such that no certain boundaries or demarcations exist between one's own spirit or awareness and the Awareness of God and sense of God's presence. The Spirit is experienced as essential to the self. It is the self at the profoundest level of who I am, where I can no longer distinguish between myself and that which is greater than I. In his *Confessions* Augustine yielded to God "more inward than my inmost part and higher than the highest element within me."

That sense of closeness can, of course, lead to questions about the reality of the experience and whether one may be in dialogue with just oneself. In the movie *The Ruling Class*, Peter O'Toole is asked, "How do you know that you are God?" "Because," he answers as a genuine nonrealist, "when I am praying, I find that I am talking to myself." From time to time, people at prayer may ask themselves whether that is what they are doing.

Even at best the kinship between human awareness and the divine would not be an experience easy to fathom or explain. At times it may seem so intimate as to be indecipherable. Although one may find personal characteristics in God, human creatures do not relate with God as though God were another being or thing in the universe whose existence one could point to and demonstrate.

The Bible can speak of God as "not far from each one of us, . . . 'in him we live and move and have our being'" (Acts 17:27–28). God is "above all" but also "through all and in all" (Ephesians 4:6). This is, in fact, one of the oldest religious understandings. "The Spirit," we read in the Mundaka Upanishad of Hinduism, "is the supreme abode wherein dwells all that moves and breathes and sees." Prayer would not, then, be a matter of sending messages over a distance—to God far away. One does not so much pray *to* the Spirit as *in* the Spirit—in the Awareness of God. The Awareness, in this sense, would be something like the air around us. The relationship is like our breath with the air. It is not surprising that "breath," "air," and "wind" are familiar ways of talking about Spirit in the Bible and in other religious and spiritual traditions. The poet George Herbert described prayer as "God's breath in man."

Meister Eckhart, a mystical theologian who lived some seven hundred years ago, was thought by some to be a heretic because of his attempts to express the inexpressible. "God is more intimately present to all creatures," he taught, "than the creature to itself. God is in the innermost depths of the soul. My truest I is God. Nothing is nearer to the soul than God." Centuries later Friedrich von Hügel wrote, "Spirit and spirit, God and the creature are not two material bodies, of which one can only be where the other is not; but, on the contrary, as regards to our own spirit, God's Spirit ever works in closest penetration and stimulation of our own; just as in return, we cannot find God's Spirit simply separate from our own spirit within ourselves."

This Awareness, often unrecognized and invisible, like the air around us, might be thought of as more the context for life than any separate entity. It might be likened to the energy of the emptiness of space that may nevertheless help give mass to the subatomic universe. It would be all the potentialities of the inhering Spirit, the ground of being that enables the universe to be and links all into relationship.

Unsayable and Saying

"My me is God," exclaimed the mystic Catherine of Genoa. "Nor do I know my selfhood save in God." Others have described their experience as more a sense of being known than of knowing—of being in the context of being known more than an experience of the ability to know something about God. More than God's presence to them is their presence with God, and it may become a relationship akin to loving.

Yet one continues to struggle to find words for what is at once a sense of intimacy so profound as not to be sure how this is more than self, while experienced within a sense of context that is greater than self and mysteriously other. The nearness is also beyond. So the author of *The Cloud of Unknowing* advised: "For God is your being, and what you are you are in God . . . because in you God is both the cause and reason for your existence . . . never forgetting, of course, this difference: that God is your being, and not you God's." God is other, while still at the same time and in spite of efforts to see the self with awareness as separate, there comes at least to many an intuition of a setting, an environment necessary for human awareness to be. Human awareness is within and depends on greater Awareness. There is Spirit that is prior, beyond, and yet the immanent context of our awareness.

Words again stumble. We are known to be knowing. We are seen that we can see. There is Awareness in which we are aware and of which we may sometimes be aware. George Steiner comes close to prayer as he reflects on the longing that is kindled when a sense of greater presence is missing, "the density of God's absence, the edge of presence in that absence." Steiner does battle with secular language to deny the deconstruction of all meaning. Ultimately, for being to be, there must be some manner of *logos*—a form or forms of rationality at the root of existence: unsayable but present, hoped for and guessed at as presences that allow that limited sayability of existence. They are, Steiner suggests again, most heard and appreciated in the music that "puts our being as men and women in touch with that which transcends the sayable, which outstrips the analyzable."

Steiner's own words, and more familiar religious language, are at best near to poetry. It is not surprising that, like poets, mystics have used the imagery of light (that still mysterious, invisible universal energy that enables being seen and us to see) to intimate how human awareness may be participant in the light of divine Awareness. In the Hindu Vedas, "the light that shines beyond this heaven, beyond all, in the highest worlds beyond which there are none higher, is truly the same light that shines within the person." Such imagery becomes metaphor—pointing to what can be alluded to but not fully said or described. It tries to suggest how Presence might be inferred to exist even though it cannot be comprehended. It is of me and more than me; self and more than self. It is the edge of presence in absence, awareness that cannot be without Awareness—the Context for life. Here are the presences and Presence that let life be, the radiance, the music, the dancing.

Sheer Silence

I have come to appreciate the diverse ways in which others in many cultures have sensed themselves to be in the presence of the divine Spirit. A variety of images and words are used, if they are even able to articulate the experience. Stories are told of sudden, dramatic moments in which persons find themselves in the presence of God's Spirit. Or a growing sensibility and quieter ways may come, in which one becomes aware of being in the Awareness. There is a sense of Awareness greater than one's own, even as individuals are left probing and wondering what this means for their lives. Sometimes in such meetings, individuals are brought to a new or renewed awareness of themselves and their mission or calling in life.

One of these individuals was a man named Elijah, who, in the days of ancient Israel, believed himself called to be a prophet for God. There came a time, however, when things were not going at all well for him. Elijah was lonely, afraid, and out of sorts. The people were following after false gods, and the forces of wrong were winning. "It is enough; now, O LORD, take away my life, for I am no better than my ancestors" (1 Kings 19:4). The prophet feels very sorry for himself: "I alone am left, and they are seeking my life, to take it away" (19:10).

Prodded by angelic messengers, Elijah flees to the mount of Horeb. Wondering and uncertain, he hopes that in that sacred space, he might experience again God's presence and calling to him. How might this be known?

> Now there was a great wind, so strong that it was splitting mountains and breaking rocks in pieces before the Lord, but the Lord was not in the wind; and after the wind an earthquake, but the Lord was not in the earthquake; and after the earthquake a fire, but the Lord was not in the fire; and after the fire a sound of sheer silence. When Elijah heard it, he wrapped his face in his mantle and went out and stood at the entrance of the cave. (1 Kings 19:11–13)

It is in that silence that a voice comes to Elijah, renewing his awareness of God's presence and his mission.

I cannot claim that I have heard distinct words in my life. Few of us probably have. But I have been in that sheer, far-from-empty, and awesome silence. I have stood with my face wrapped in my mantle when there is nothing I can see or say. I have felt myself known more than any knowing. There I have heard something like voices, sometimes mingled with my own and sometimes perhaps not—whispers, a kind of music. There has been a profound and moving sense of Presence and relationship.

Who Is Jesus?

The best-known individual who is said to have profoundly experienced the Spirit of God in his life is Jesus of Nazareth. Because I was raised as a Christian, I heard from an early age the stories about Jesus: the poor family with no place to stay, the shepherds and wise men at his birth, the healing of a blind man. I heard about his casting out evil spirits, his feeding five thousand people with a few loaves of bread and fishes, and his walking on water. I listened to his parables of the good Samaritan and prodigal son, of a dinner party where the invited guests did not come and the riffraff of the city were welcome. I heard stories of sowing and reaping, of sheep and shepherds, of masters and servants, of a last supper, and of his betrayal, tortured death, and then living again.

As a child I was a participant in the pageants that retold the Christmas and Epiphany stories. At six or seven I was a shepherd or a wise man—a king dressed in my bathrobe with a kind of turban that someone's mother had made. I held out before me a beautifully wrapped box that, by shaking, I could tell was actually empty. Solemnly I walked up the church's center aisle while the congregation sang "We Three Kings of Orient Are." I then piped up in my little voice, "Frankincense to offer have I: incense owns a Deity nigh"—whatever that meant. The narrator next described how the wise men, after refusing to return and inform King Herod where the child lay, went off to their own country "by another way." We little kings, after kneeling down to the doll baby Jesus and leaving our boxes, stole out of the sanctuary through the side door.

When I was a bit older, I got to be the pious Joseph, who never had anything to say. The next year, as the wicked Herod, I had some great lines: "Go and search diligently for the child; and when you have found him, bring me word that I may also go and pay him homage." *Heh! Heh! Heh!* Why, I have come to wonder, did that part seem the most fun?

Through the Church year, we sang other hymns: "Fairest Lord Jesus" and "Sacred Head Sore Wounded." Some of the stories and hymns left me awestruck. They seemed beautiful and full of meaning. Others puzzled me, or I thought them rather strange.

Who was this Jesus? I soon realized that there had to be more here than met the eye—both in the sense that some of the stories about Jesus could not have happened in the way they were described, and that his message and the meaning of his life and death had to be more complicated and profound than "Fairest Lord Jesus" let on. I was beginning to realize the differences between what could be surmised about the Jesus of history and the Jesus of faith, or the Church Jesus. I wanted to know more about the relationship between them. Above all, it was the stories of Jesus and about Jesus that fascinated me, and the best way, I think I already intuited, to relate to Jesus.

Probably most of us do not plan out our lives. I certainly did not. After theological studies and ordination as a priest in the Episcopal Church, I thought I would use my life as a pastor. But I continued to be drawn to being a teacher, and so after more study, found myself teaching undergraduates and then those training to be pastors and future teachers. Students and teachers alike went through a kind of second wave of interest in the historical Jesus. The first wave had ended with scholars like Albert Schweitzer and then Rudolph Bultmann, who overturned the late-nineteenth-century historical optimism that scientific, historical study could result in access to the Jesus who had lived amid the hills and by the sea in what came to be called the Holy Land. It was, however, Bultmann's students who developed approaches that again led to a renewed optimism that historians might establish a core of sayings and actions that would give a picture of the historical Jesus. After that hope began to be severely questioned (not least because of the different pictures that emerged), a kind of third wave came along that used sociological insights, archeological information, and more recently discovered gospels and purported sayings of Jesus. There continues to be a spate of books about the historical Jesus. Yet, although there was now some better information about the period (including the Dead Sea Scrolls), and Jesus could be better set in the Jewish context of the time, the so-called historical Jesus seemed to many to still be an elusive figure, too far back in history and too colored by the believers' understandings of him to emerge with clarity.

I poignantly remember a first trip to the Holy Land and vividly not finding any signs of the historical Jesus there. One could see something of the work of Herod in ancient ruins and trace bits of the history of earlier Judaism and the later Crusades, but of Jesus there was nothing, no physical remnant of anything he had done, other than some fought-over and rather commercialized guesses about the places of his birth and Crucifixion and the location of the empty tomb. Only when I came to Lake Galilee, saw a fishing boat, and looked out on the waves ruffled by the wind, did I imagine I could see something of what he had seen and what life had been like for him.

As a teacher and theologian, I also had to reckon with the fact that the Bible was in words. From somewhere in young adulthood, I remember hearing an adage about scripture that stuck with me: "The Bible is in the world as Jesus was in the world." Just as the human being Jesus was participant in all human limitations on knowing and understanding, so was and is the Bible. From my studies of literature and work as a poet, I knew that words are slippery things. They are at best approximations. They point to realities they are trying to describe. In its use of hymn, poetry, sign, symbol, and sacrament, the Church in which I came to serve and work seemed to me to see the Bible as a kind of sacrament. At its best, rather than containing some form of inerrant truth, its words and stories gestured through human yearning toward God's presence and guidance in life. The Bible, too, was about keeping the deepest questions of human life in sometimes agonizing searches for God in contexts where the true enemy of faith was not doubt or struggle but false religion and human pretense and religiosity. I heard the psalmist ask God, "Why do you hide yourself in times of trouble?" (Psalm 10:1). I heard Job wondering, "Why is light given to one in misery?" (Job 3:20) and recognized his questions as acts of faith, as was Jesus' haunting "My God, my God, why have you forsaken me?" (Mark 15:34).

That is how scripture, with all its outdated understandings (including its stories of tribal warfare and blood and cruelty with even God said to be joining in), came alive. Scripture became animate as a human story of people seeking to understand their relationship with God. The one consistent message about God throughout the Bible is that God is, on the one hand, a God of holiness and justice and, on the other hand, a God of extraordinary forgiveness and generosity. Righteousness and mercy are both of God in ways humans can never fully understand. This frequent both/and rather than either/or of scripture (Jesus can say "the road is hard" [Matthew 7:14] and "my burden is light" [11:30]) reminds me of the surprises of quantum physics and of light active as both wave and particle. In the Bible it can best be heard in the narrative structure through which scripture often communicates, with its many stories of judgment and mercy, losing and finding, longing hope and challenge, tragedy, repentance, forgiveness, and new life.

Divine Awareness with Jesus

Early in his ministry, Jesus came to the Jordan River to be baptized with water by one known as John the Baptist. As he was coming up out of the river, the story goes, the heavens opened and the Spirit of God descended upon him like a dove. A voice was then heard from heaven, "You are my Son, the Beloved; with you I am well pleased" (Mark 1:11).

This story as presented in Mark's Gospel can be understood as a kind of adoption of a human person to be God's Son. The revelation is made directly to Jesus. In the story as told in Matthew's Gospel, the voice offers more of a public pronouncement—a disclosure to others of who Jesus is: "This is my Son, the Beloved, with whom I am well pleased" (Matthew 3:17).

Among Jesus' first disciples, one of the earliest ways of understanding Jesus both as human and as God was to see him as a human person who had the Spirit of God. The Gospel of Luke particularly stresses this understanding of Jesus and his ministry. Luke tells the story of the Spirit coming upon Jesus at his baptism, but earlier Luke also envisions the Spirit present at Jesus' conception. The angel Gabriel announces to Mary, "The Holy Spirit will come upon you, and the power of the Most High will overshadow you" (Luke 1:35). To put it too simply, it is as though Jesus was human from birth through Mary while another part of him was of the Holy Spirit.

The presence of the Spirit continues to be with Jesus in Luke's Gospel. Often he is seen at prayer. After the Holy Spirit descended upon him at the baptism, he is described as "full of the Holy Spirit." Then he "was led by the Spirit in the wilderness, where for forty days he was tempted by the devil" (Luke 4:1–2). Following his temptation, and "filled with the power of the Spirit," Jesus returned to Galilee (4:14). There, in a synagogue on the sabbath day, he unrolled the scroll of the prophet Isaiah and read from it: "The Spirit of the Lord is upon me, / because he has anointed me / to bring good news to the poor" (4:18). Later in his ministry, after the seventy disciples have returned from their mission, "Jesus rejoiced in the Holy Spirit" as he gave thanks to God (10:21).

After the Resurrection Paul provided another variation on the theme when he wrote of "[God's] Son, who was descended from David according to the flesh and was declared to be Son of God with power according to the spirit of holiness by resurrection from the dead" (Romans 1:3–4). Again, Jesus is presented in his humanity with the Spirit of God acting in his life.

On into the early centuries of the Church, people wrestled with their understandings of how Jesus could be fully a human being and yet have divine life present within him. The strongest encouragement for this faith that Jesus was both human and of God was not elaborate theological thinking but a profound sensibility on the part of suffering and hoping human beings. If Jesus was to be their savior, God had to have been present with Jesus. And this had to be truly God—not some angel or other heavenly being. On the other hand, to be their savior, Jesus also needed to have lived completely a human life. He had to be wholly a human being—not only with flesh and bones but also with all the human emotions and mentality, and surely also with a human awareness and spirit. Other ideas were tried, but it finally would not do to have him be God dressed up in a human suit or pretending to be human—something like Clark Kent, knowing he could change into Superman whenever he needed to.

When I think about Jesus and his humanity, I see him first as someone like us—"like his brother and sisters," as the Letter to the Hebrews puts it, "in every respect" (2:17). He, too, started life as a baby. He was born, however else his nativity is to be understood, in the heat and blood and passion of human birth. His all-too-human death was also to be one of blood and agony.

As Jesus grew and matured, he would have learned to make a living, possibly in his father's trade as a carpenter. I can imagine long hours at a bench learning those skills, perhaps one day bleeding on the wood as a knife or chisel slipped. I can imagine him limited in his knowledge by the geography and understandings of his circumstances—a child and then a man of his own particular culture and time. I think of him having times of uncertainty and awe, and I can imagine days in his life of prayer when the divine Spirit was intimate with him—Jesus becoming more and more aware of God's calling and presence.

Every human being is able to have an awareness of self, and with it personhood, language, story, responsibility, and love. One can wonder about how with this awareness they may find a relationship with the divine Awareness or Spirit of God. This is a way of understanding human beings as related to God or, as the Bible speaks of the relationship, being in the *image* of God. In this kinship there may be moments when the self aware and the divine Awareness draw close. "My me is God," we remember Catherine of Genoa exclaiming. "My truest I is God," taught Meister Eckhart. "Nothing is nearer to the soul than God." "For God is your being," wrote the author of *The Cloud of Unknowing*, "and what you are you are in God." This language, with its mystical dimensions, is also based in human experience echoed in a number of times and cultures. It does also seem that the Awareness, intimate to all life, is closer to the awareness of some persons than others.

It is in this way that one may think of the divine Spirit having been especially present with the life of a particular human being. In Jesus' person the character of God's Awareness—not least in its self-giving, sacrificial character—may be glimpsed. In him the theater of inner human awareness was also lit with the light of divine Awareness. This may be, as well, a way of interpreting the experiences that lie behind stories like those of the baptism and Jesus' transfiguration and the intimacy of Jesus calling on God as *Abba*, like a child's almost-babbling word for parent—Dada, Daddy, Father.

God's Ways in Person

His disciples remembered Jesus as the one who had taught about God's ways—God's ways of being present, of being sovereign—what Jesus called the kingdom of God. Those ways, he said, were already begun. Although they were to be better known in the future, they did not represent a distant place nor were they far off in some hereafter. They already approaching from God's future. They were already a possibility in human life: "Your kingdom come . . . on earth as it is in heaven" (Matthew 6:10). "The kingdom of God is among you" (Luke 17:21).

These ways were the ways of peace—a peace that is the fullness of rightness and justice. "Blessed are the peacemakers" (Matthew 5:9). "Blessed are those who hunger and thirst for righteousness, for they will be filled" (5:6). Blessing comes upon those who mourn and are merciful, upon the humble in heart and spirit who do not put themselves first in life (see Matthew 5:3–9). Those who would be first are to be in the service of others (see Mark 10:43–44).

Although I continued to be aware of all the historical and critical problems involved in gaining any knowledge of Jesus as a historical person, I did feel I could have some sense of his personality—especially through the stories he told. They suggest he was quite a character. His stories even have a certain mischievousness about them. Since the God he professed was a God of both demanding righteousness and almost unbelievable compassion, the ways of God would have to be full of surprises—sometimes upending human ideas about who was good and who was bad and where mercy and love and true fairness could be found. People who worked for only an hour would be paid the same as those who had worked for twelve. The prodigal son would be grandly welcomed home, while the hardworking elder brother pouted out in the field. The poor, lame, and blind would feast at the dinner party when the invited guests did not come. As long as selfishness and greed, suffering and death, seemed to be so dominant in the world, it is almost comic of Jesus to insist that God's ways of justice and peace were what ultimately mattered.

The early followers of Jesus tried to describe their understanding of him by giving him various titles and designations. They took these from their traditions and the longing of those before them. He is seen as a great teacher, or rabbi, and also a prophet led by God's Spirit. There was speculation that he was the promised prophet who would come at the end of the age or to be the new Moses. He was also associated with the prophesied figure who was God's servant, the suffering one who was said to be "oppressed" and "afflicted." "He was despised. . . . We held him of no account. . . . He has borne our infirmities. . . . He was wounded for our transgressions . . . and by his bruises we are healed. . . . The righteous one, my servant, shall make many righteous" (Isaiah 53:3–11).

Jesus is called the anointed one, the Christ, who is chosen by God and who will take up King David's rule, or the role of other anointed figures, in a new age for God's people. He is the Lord, a title which at one level is an address of respect, but at another was also used for God and came, therefore, to be used in worship of Jesus.

Jesus is both Son of God and Son of Man. The latter is a title that has engendered competing theories among New Testament scholars. Son of Man can refer to a human being or a special human being and also one like a human being who comes from the heavenly realms to bring judgment and the beginning of the new age. Son of God, despite the seemingly divine ring to the title, was more a way of designating a human chosen or adopted by God to represent God's ruling presence in the world.

In later Christian reflection and worship, Jesus could be called the one who saves, the Savior, a title more in use in the Greco-Roman cultures beyond Judaism. In the opening of the Gospel of John, he is represented as the *Logos,* or Word of God—the operative expression of divine creativity that out of the potentiality of God's imagination brought all things into being. A letter written to the early Church in the city of Colossae uses language associated with both *Logos* and Wisdom. These were figures seen, in Jewish thought of the time, as living attributes of God, vital to the creation and sustenance of the world. So we hear that "He was in the beginning with God. All things came into being through him" (John 1:2–3). "He is the image of the invisible God . . . for in him all things in heaven and on earth were created" (Colossians 1:15–16).

Just as important as any titles, however, were the stories of and about Jesus. In the understanding of his time, he heals people and casts out destructive spirits that are within them. He reaches out to lepers and others who are sick and outcast. He offers acceptance to those regarded as sinners or otherwise outside God's care and concern. They, too, are invited to be part of the ways of God that Jesus proclaimed had already begun in this world.

In his disciples' understanding, Jesus not only told of this invitation, he enacted it. He not only spoke God's word, but his ministry so personified it that he became God's Word to them. One of the teachers in the early Church said that Jesus had so embodied the kingdom (in Greek, *basileia*) about which he taught that he was *autobasileia*—the kingdom himself—God's ways in person. His life and stories showed forth the ways of God's holiness and mercy, justness and love, in such a manner that he in his person was the revelation of those ways. He was its incarnation; in

Shakespeare's phrase, he was able to "body forth" the *way* of God. He was God's parable. His words about coming "not to be served but to serve" (Mark 10:45) offered a revelation about the character of the divine Spirit in human life. In him the Spirit of all life and the human spirit were met.

After Jesus' death, the disciples continued to feel close to the Spirit or Awareness of God. It reminded them of Jesus. The Spirit was to them Jesus-like. In their immediate experience, it was as though Jesus was still with them. One imagines them at a meal, reminiscing about what Jesus had told them of God's ways. Had he not told them that love's ways must also lead to suffering? They read over the prophet's words that spoke of one who "was despised and rejected . . . struck down by God, and afflicted . . . wounded for our transgressions" and yet "by his bruises we are healed" (Isaiah 53:3–5). Someone retold the story of Jesus offering forgiveness and new hope to a paralyzed young man. They recalled how the young man got up from his bed and found new life. Another disciple then recalled Jesus' story about a dinner party where life's poor and injured were welcomed. They smiled to one another and now poured their own wine and broke their bread as he had done with them. Had he not said, "This is my body" and "This is my blood"?

In the Gospel of John, the Spirit is presented as a kind of successor to Jesus, coming after his death and Resurrection. The experience of this Spirit of God brings comfort, hope, and challenge in Jesus' name. This Spirit "will take what is mine and declare it to you" (John 16:15). The Spirit will both remind the disciples of Jesus and be their way of knowing that the Spirit, who was with Jesus, is still alive with them. This Gospel describes an intimacy of love and abiding between the Spirit and Jesus and God as Father, into which the disciples are invited to join through their relationship with the Spirit, now best known to them in Jesus.

Elsewhere in the New Testament, the Spirit can be spoken of as though a third *person*, but is also said to be the Spirit of Jesus and the Spirit of God. Sometimes, it would appear, this can be done quite interchangeably. In one passage, Paul speaks of the Spirit of God that dwells in the disciples, the Spirit of the One who raised Jesus from the dead, the Spirit of Christ, and the Spirit that leads the children of God (see Romans

8:9–17). In the Acts of the Apostles, Jesus, after being raised up and receiving from the Father the promise of the Holy Spirit, pours this out upon his disciples (see 1:5–2:36).

Not Confined

Christians have always wanted to share with others their belief in this special experience of the divine Awareness in Jesus. Perhaps what was and is most important to them is that they offer their faith that the love and servant character of God's Spirit was present in Jesus' Passion and death. So does the cross become a forever sign of God's participation in a cross-shaped world. This compassion and reconciling love is the intrinsic character of the Spirit of all life.

This is a faith that can be shared, however, without needing to place limitations on the presence of divine Awareness in other faiths and persons. The Spirit of all life, I have come to believe, is far greater than any human ways of understanding or credence, however noble. To say that God's Spirit is best defined by Jesus is not to say that God's Spirit is confined to Jesus. It is not limited to him. The Bible and the writings of other religions suggest that all human life is made in the image of God. Every human being has the potential, through self-awareness, for relationship with the Spirit of all life. In other faiths and experiences, the Awareness may be appreciated in different words, symbols, and stories. It may be the Great Spirit, known in much Native American life and faith. It may be the Brahman of Hinduism, reverenced as the absolute underlying of all the workings of the universe. With this Brahman, the *atman*, or innermost self, in all beings can be in relationship, even participating in Brahman so that mystical unity is found without loss of self. Brahman is the light of all the universe in which the light of human self-awareness may come to share. This light comes from the "Storehouse of the Great Light" of Buddhist teaching.

The Spirit of God is, of course, known throughout Judaism in its scriptures and life. The creative renewing *ruach* is the Spirit moving in the creation and the wind-Spirit that also inspires the prophets. "The Spirit of the Lord GOD is upon me / because the LORD has anointed me," announced the prophet Isaiah (Isaiah 61:1). It is the Spirit that came to Elijah in the silence. The Spirit does not need to be made present, for it can be everywhere. Fleeing from his brother's anger, Jacob awakes from his dream to realize, "Surely the Lord is in this place—and I did not know it!" (Genesis 28:16). "Where can I go from your Spirit?" the psalmist asks, "Or where can I flee from your presence?" (Psalm 139:7).

> If I take the wings of the morning
>> and settle at the farthest limits of the sea,
> even there your hand shall lead me,
>> and your right hand shall hold me fast.
>
> (Psalm 139:9–10)

Reflecting on the God of the prophets and God's people's experience, Jewish theologian Abraham Heschel wrote of the Spirit of God that suffers with the people of God—the divine pathos. In almost every religion, the empathy of God is realized. Nor is spirit language "abstract language about a vague God, elusive and far removed," discerns Diane Eck. "On the contrary, it is intimate language." And light and fire, fountain and stream of life, wind and breath, are ways of alluding to the presence of the Spirit of God in all of life.

Modesty in the Spirit

Among the important commonalties at the heart of many faiths is an attractive modesty. While often claiming to offer a supreme understanding of God or reality, at the core of their theology and in their scriptures, these faiths allude to the elusiveness of God in terms of the inability of human words or comprehension to know or describe God's ways in any sense fully. They even recognize how formalized religion can become a barrier to relationship with the true God—the God behind God, as it were. "My thoughts are not your thoughts, nor are your ways my ways," says the Lord of Israel (Isaiah 55:8). "The Tao that can be named is not the eternal Tao," maintained Lao-tzu, known as the founder of Taoism. "I AM WHO I AM," God responds to Moses' request for God's name (Exodus 3:14). The God of all life—the God of absolute righteousness and loving mercy—is not in the control of human naming or words.

All major religions also espouse a form of the golden rule in its positive and negative forms, based, as we have seen, in a developed awareness of self and others. "As I am so are they; as they are so am I" is one of the teachings of Buddhism. "In everything do to others as you would have them do to you," Jesus taught (Matthew 7:12). Many faiths base their morality and sense of the goal of human life in a transformation from self-centeredness to a centeredness that values love and compassion above all. "Those who kill a life, it is as if they killed the whole human civilization. And those who save a life, it is as if they saved the whole civilization," pronounces the Qu'ran. Common to them all is care for the poor.

Together religions, including many of the world's newly forming and always-changing religions, recognize the tragic character of life with its suffering and death, while finding in suffering a deepened spirituality and believing yet that God or ultimate reality is good. At the heart of all life is the compassionate wisdom of God, the principle of rightness known variously as Dharma, Rta, and Tao in eastern religions. Indeed, it is a deepened participation in divine Awareness that may most help one to sense how others find comfort, challenge, sustenance, and hope in their faith and in their ways of prayer, meditation, and worship. Over the years I have had some tough experiences in dialogue with those of different faiths—not least in the company of Christians from others parts of the world where Christianity is a minority religion. In such conversations, one recognizes again how deeply and inevitably a particular religion is enmeshed with the values of its culture and can let itself be defined by local politics, economics, and personal power trips. Every religion may fall under the spell of the fear of others who are different. Religions can be and have been used to separate peoples and for cruelty and oppression. I have come to hope that we may, nonetheless, learn that what we most have to share with one another is not so much religion as it is the presence of the divine Spirit in life—a faith put pungently in the bumper sticker "My karma ran over your dogma," or when the Sufi poet Rumi maintains that the lovers of God have no religion but God alone.

Just as a garden may have many different plants and trees that are watered from the same well, so may many peoples draw upon this same Spirit. Close friendships may be formed with people of other faiths when the third participant in the friendship is the Spirit appreciated in the quest for the goodness—for truth and beauty in life. I think particularly of the friendships of the Hindu Mohandas Gandhi with Muslims and Christians. Despite human failing and the misuse of much religion, there may come a recognition that life's greatest gifts are what all people may know through relationship with divine Awareness: the *ahimsa* or "do no harm" of Hinduism and Jainism; the "sympathy with all things" of Buddhism; the fruit of the Spirit of God: "love, joy, peace, patience, kindness, generosity, faithfulness, gentleness, and self-control" (Galatians 5:22–23). There may then come recognition of opportunities to care together for a shared fairness in life, for the peacefulness of reconciliation, and for the planet itself.

Four &8 In the Suffering

Sam and the Interfaith Council

Trusting that the Spirit of all life is experienced in many faiths, I gathered together, during the years when I was a university chaplain, a group of students from different religious backgrounds. We called it the Interfaith Council and, not knowing what else to do, began meeting in my home once a month for supper and conversation. Because students like food and meeting from time to time in a home, it seemed to work.

Although I had not planned it that way, food also became one of our major conversation topics. The students asked to take over the preparation of the meals and cooked from their own traditions: Greek Orthodox, Middle Eastern Arabic, intercontinental Baha'i, Indian, Italian Catholic, Ghanaian, Jewish, Chinese. The orthodox Jewish students brought their own food or ate before or after our meetings. We talked about what people could and could not eat and the significance of food and food preparations in their cultures and religions.

This experience led us to realize that we could also take on such topics as scripture, time, money, music, prayer, family, sexuality, success, and failure and talk about them from the perspective of the several faith traditions. Because the students were bright and generally well informed about their religions, we had some invigorating conversations, and considerable learning took place. More and more we found ourselves taking on and keeping what we came to refer as life's "Big Questions."

Samiran was one of the brightest, with an infectious smile that lit up his dark face and a friendliness that went with the smile and drew other students to him. One day in his senior year, Sam borrowed a van to pick up some films for a club he belonged to. Not that familiar with New Jersey dual highways, Sam somehow turned the van into the path of a semitrailer truck.

Sam's parents and sister came from India and, though Hindus, asked me to conduct the memorial service. All the members of the Interfaith Council came to the liturgy. Our devastated council found that it had another profound question with which to deal.

Given our faith that the divine Spirit is compassionate and wise, I and every other would-be believer has yet had to contend with all that seems to be so tragic in life. We live in a world of love and beauty, but where terrible things happen to every kind of people. Every religion and everyone who hopes in the ultimate goodness of God and life must struggle with all that seems to go wrong, and the more aware a creature becomes of the world about it, the greater would seem to become the awareness of pain and suffering. It is painful enough when harsh things happen to creatures with little awareness. I felt awful for my dog, Sydney, when he tore open his leg while out running one day. But tragedy seems multiplied for those who are fully aware of their lives and deaths, of suffering and love. With greater awareness comes the potential for a greater empathy and sharing in the pain and suffering of others. The more aware one is, the more life can hurt. Here is reason, as we have seen, not to want too much awareness, or at least to try to dull it.

If it is true of us that the more we are aware, the more suffering there is, one can only try to imagine the suffering of the divine Awareness. At times in my prayers or when I am awake at night, I do imagine that I can hear something of the pain and fear. I again hold Sam's father's hand. My colleague and the pastor of the church where my family worships is senselessly shot in a botched robbery, and I am asked to preach to his family and friends at his funeral. A child is born with an incurable malady. A prisoner is brutally tortured to death. Our earth is energetic and changing, but this means that monsoons sweep away whole villages. Earthquakes, like the terrifying shaking that badly damaged our house and many churches in Los Angeles, crush people's homes on top of them. A tectonic plate shifts far beneath the surface of the Indian Ocean, and the resulting tsunami takes the lives of as many as two hundred thousand children and their parents and grandparents. Meanwhile, the plane goes out of control. I hear the screaming and terror. A war ends, but the horrors continue: a landmine blows off a child's leg, refugees scavenge for food, African grandparents care for their AIDS-orphaned grandchildren who are also dying of AIDS, a girl is sold into a life of prostitution by impoverished relatives, an elderly woman agonizes alone with a painful cancer. There is the loss of a loved mate, a father accidentally backs his car over his beloved child, a depressed teenager holds a gun in his hand.

I cannot stand to do this for very long. I am, however, left with an aching in my heart and a wish to imagine some theodicy—a way there can be a good God and yet all the suffering. Could there be reason or at least some rhyme to bring peace and reconciliation with the ways of creation?

Perilous Beauty

I turn in the Bible to a story Jesus told. He described a sower who sowed seeds in a way often used then. Instead of plowing the field first, the sower casts the seeds about. The seeds end up in a variety of circumstances. In a version of the parable that may be reconstructed from the several gospels, we notice a strong triadic, almost musical character. Following the introduction are three scenes of loss before the final one of growth. All the scenes have their own three-part structure:

> Now a sower went out to sow, and
> it happened in the sowing that
> > some fell by the path, and the birds
> came, and ate it.
> > And others fell on rocky ground, and the

sun arose, and scorched it.
    And others fell among the thorns, and the
thorns grew up, and choked it
    And others fell on good soil, and
brought forth grain, and yielded
thirty-fold and sixty-fold and one hundred fold.

On one hearing this is an optimistic story—even a kind of resurrection story. Stress and considerable loss happen in life, but in the end comes abundance. Whether the thirty, sixty, or a hundredfold refers to the grains in different ears or grains from different parts of the field, the growth can seem a splendid, natural produce, and it may also allude to a more miraculous result.

In any case, much of the story is true to nature. Nature's generous profligacy keeps life going and may many times produce abundance, but at a price. Farming, as many of life's other ventures, is costly. Full crops may be harvested but much is regularly lost along the way. The parable seems to emphasize the almost violent character of what can happen: the birds, sun and thorns *attack* the seeds. I remember once going to a meeting that took place on an Iowa farm. I had a picture in my head of Iowa farmers who were conservative in their habits and ways. As the conversation went on, however, I realized that a number of the farmers there had recently returned from a junket to Las Vegas. Puzzled by this I asked a friend to explain. "You must realize," he said, "that all farmers are gamblers. They have to be. Sometimes the crops come in pretty well, but other years there's drought. Some years there are wet fields in the spring and bugs and blight of all kinds. Some years they may go belly up."

There are other ventures in life that are not unlike this—from fishing to mining to the stock market. The great African-American ballplayer Satchel Paige, who was finally allowed to pitch in the major leagues when he was in his forties, put it well: "Some days you win; some days you lose; some days you get rained out."

We may marvel that so much good comes in life—that there is so much good and beauty. But along the way, there seems to be enormous waste and cost as well. Why so much profusion and diversity: a hundred billion galaxies for perhaps a relatively few planets with life, thousands of seeds for one tree, millions of sperm for one birth? There are now six billion human lives on the planet. We think, too, of all the lives before us including all the prehumans and protohumans and human ancestors, many of whom lived short, brutish lives. To produce us? And are we, in reality, but the cogs—the gene containers for the next billions?

The evolutionary process is dynamic and wondrous in the complexity, fecundity, and diversity of its results. It is, as it were, always experimenting, trying new combinations of genes and compounds, often using the seemingly odd and abnormal to see what might work next. Within it may be inbuilt a bias and uptick toward more complexity—perhaps even to more consciousness and awareness. But the process itself can seem blind and full of cruelty and waste as it blunders on. Charles Darwin could look out on a field and take in the beauty of flowers and insects, but he also knew what was going on below sight—the constant hunting, killing, and eating—the diseases, pain, and little screams of dying lives. Darwin was not one to want to trouble the faith of believers in God, but was himself troubled and uncertain: "What a book a Devil's chaplain might write on the clumsy, wasteful, blundering low and horridly cruel works of nature!" Although impressed by the ingenuity with which species adapt and become more efficient hunters, I grow sick of all the catching and digesting of the Animal Planet and National Geographic television programs. If nothing else, think of what the African guinea worm parasite does once it gets into people's bodies. I thought about it in a poem:

> The ordered stage we were told to watch,
> with chance the outlaw actor,
> while now we see in every scene
> the accidental factor.
> Without random's role then stasis' rule
> would have creation frozen;
> as surely it's necessity
> upholding all that's chosen.

Not only once, but at every edge,
as chaos threatens ever,
bits link, shape life, they end and eat
where strange attractors gather.
There's tense interplay among the ways,
in the flow to entropy,
mere principles in subtle sets
gender vast complexity.
And in the joining, in the struggle,
as the smarter, stronger form,
in the suffering, in the learning,
perilous beauty is born.

The Long Line of Questions

All the good that creation produces may be seen as perilously beautiful, but is it sufficient when placed on the scales against all the suffering and evil? Is it all worthwhile, including the pain and death of nature's carnage?

Long ago this was one of the questions Job and the friends who came to reason with him asked—with mixed results. In one disaster after another, Job had lost his children, his home and possessions, and then his health. At the end of his rope and hope, Job curses the day of his birth and laments in one long *why*:

> Why did I not die at birth,
>   come forth from the womb and expire?
>   . . . .
> Or why was I not buried like a stillborn child,
>   like an infant that never sees the light?
> There the wicked cease from troubling,
>   and there the weary are at rest.
>   . . . .
> Why is light given to one in misery,
>   and life to the bitter in soul?
>   (Job 3:11,16–17,20)

Job, however, persists in his inquiry as to why there should be human life and awareness, and finally he has his longed-for encounter with God. But the questions of the Book of Job regarding life's tragic character and fairness live on. Throughout the Bible, as the people who believe themselves chosen by God experience calamity after calamity, when the kingdom does not come, when Jesus is put to death, when, after his death, Jerusalem is destroyed and many people are slaughtered, desperate questions are asked of God. A woman once told her pastor that when she got to heaven, she wanted to get in line to ask God about all the bad things that had happened in her life. "Ma'am," the pastor responded, "it's a very long line."

Many attempts have been made at answers or partial answers. The creation has been likened to a great symphony in which some sounds, heard on their own, may seem discordant and ugly, but one must pay attention to the overall beauty of the symphony. More subtle and appealing is Mary Oliver's poem "Praise":

Knee-deep
  in the ferns
    springing up
      at the edge of the whistling swamp
I watch the owl
  with its satisfied,
    heart-shaped face
      as it flies over the water—
back and forth—
  as it flutters down
    like a hellish moth
      wherever the reeds twitch—
Whenever, in the muddy cover,
  some little life sighs
    before it slides into the moonlight
      and becomes a shadow.
In the distance,
  awful and infallible

the old swamp belches.
    Of course
it stabs my heart
    whenever something cries out
    like a teardrop.
        But isn't it wonderful
What is happening
    in the branches of the pines:
    the owl's young,
        dressed in snowflakes,
are starting to fatten—
    they beat their muscular wings,
    they dream of flying
        for another million years
over the water
    over the ferns,
        over the world's roughage
        as it bleeds and deepens.

In another poem, "The Ponds," Oliver's faith is even more clear. Somehow the interdependence and cooperation in nature all work together.

> I want to believe that the imperfections are nothing—
> that the light is everything—that it is more than the sum
> of each flawed blossom rising and fading. And I do.

Yet there lingers in one's hearing, "some little life sighs, . . . for another million years . . . as it bleeds and deepens."

Life, it has been suggested, is like a mosaic in which some of the pieces are very dark, but in which all participate in an overall design. Or it is a symphony in which some of the notes may sound harsh, but all together there is loveliness. In a cruder analogy, God is pictured as the casino owner. The house may lose some pretty big bets along the way, but the house always wins. The percentages make sure of that. Overall,

God and the creation have the winning edge.

❀

But what is to be said to the losers? All the suffering of the natural world may seem bad enough, but to it we must add the many ways in which humans can be crass and brutal to one another. What is to be said to the children born irreparably deformed, the weak ones who are pushed out of the nest? What is to be said to those whose lives are degraded and dehumanized in ways that cannot be overcome? What is to be said to the horribly abused little girl? What is to be said to the mother torn from her children and led to the gas chambers at Auschwitz, after the killing fields of Cambodia, Rwanda, and Kosovo? What is to be said: "Hope you enjoyed the symphony"? "Don't worry, the house always wins"?

In one's darker days, it is hard not to wonder about any fundamental goodness in life or even if God is all that good. When Jewish monotheism forged the several understandings of divinity into one, it was unable to take away the responsibility for evil from the one God—a God who can sometimes seem severe or punishing. From time to time God saves Israel, but look what happens to the Egyptians and the Amelekites! And, although Israel hears of God's forgiveness and love for them, along the way they experience slavery, exile, and thousands dying in the Lord's fierce retribution. From time to time, for whatever reason, the devil or evil is allowed to have its way. In what the evangelist Luke suggests is the greatest of Jesus' temptations, the devil places Jesus on the pinnacle of the temple and says to him:

> If you are the Son of God, throw yourself down from here, for
> it is written,
> "He will command his angels concerning you,
>> to protect you,"
> and
> "On their hands they will bear you up,
>> so that you will not dash your foot against a stone."
>> (Luke 4:10–11)

But how confident can we be that God—who later in the story will not save Jesus from a more gruesome death—would prevent not only Jesus' foot but all his body and brain from being dashed on the pavement below if he should jump? I may count myself lucky that I was not killed when I fell the forty feet out of a tree, but there seemed no angel to stay my fall. More than once the psalmist despairs:

> [I am] like those forsaken among the dead,
>> like the slain that lie in the grave,
> like those whom you remember no more,
>> for they are cut off from your hand.
>> . . . .
> Your wrath has swept over me;
>> your dread assaults destroy me.
>> (Psalm 88:5,16)

Not on Wednesdays and Fridays

Some of the efforts toward trying to find meaning or partial answers to such darkness recognize ways in which God may be seen as *good* but not all-powerful—or at least not able to do all things. I have imagined God growing with the universe—still, in some sense, in the process of becoming fully God. The Spirit of this God, reaching back from some consummation beyond our sense of time, must yet act within the limits of this time and creation. This, if you will, is a complex God whose being is necessary to creation but who is in some ways dependent on it. God is omnipotent as the creator but then must relate to creation within its terms. There cannot be light without darkness. God's creative love and energy may be boundless, but there cannot be square circles. Existence is inescapably compromised by its requirements. There cannot be good without evil. There cannot be love without suffering. Nor can there be some measure of human freedom without the possibility that people will be cruel and selfish. The God of the Bible certainly does not seem to get God's way every time. Far from it! Israel wanders off time and again. Prophets are ignored and murdered. Jesus is put to death.

But what good, many have asked, is a God who is so unable to set things right? "Why do you sleep, O Lord?" / "Awake," the psalmist cries out. "How long shall the wicked exult?" (Psalms 44:23, 94:3). Is God in some way absent-minded, or perhaps engaged in so much creativity in many universes that it is hard to give much attention to human creatures? If God is not all-powerful, or not yet all-powerful, can God be efficacious? Even if God is awake and aware of wrong and suffering but can do nothing about it, what good is that Awareness?

These are the questions that have helped lead to what might be called the "recession" of God in this secular age, even for many who still use God language. Impishly, while also catching the spirit of the age, Woody Allen refers to God as an "underachiever." More in sadness than in anger, Samuel Beckett, author of *Waiting for Godot*, the classic staging of divine absence, follows the implications to atheism: "He doesn't exist, the bastard." And, of course, that is the simplest and for many the easiest and best way to deal with theodicy and the problem of evil. If there is no God and source of ultimate goodness, evil and suffering just *are*. The theological or philosophical problem goes away.

❀

When I was a junior teacher on the staff of the English theological college in Birmingham, we had a regular round of morning and evening services. On most mornings we used the full service of Morning Prayer, followed by Holy Communion. But on Wednesdays and Fridays during the Lenten season, we had a special order. Morning Prayer was shortened and concluded just before the Apostles' Creed would otherwise be said. This was done so that we could instead include a series of prayers and responses called the litany in the service.

It must, therefore, have been on a Wednesday or Friday during Lent that a sleepy student leading the worship forgot the special order. When Morning Prayer should have stopped, he proceeded to introduce the creed with the words, "I believe in God . . ."

A great hush fell over the chapel. Everyone realized a mistake had been made. No one knew how to proceed. Then from the back of the chapel, the voice of the principal was heard, "Not on Wednesdays and Fridays."

The point was not lost on the theological students. Some days, at least, belief in the ultimate goodness of life and in God is far from easy. Or, even if one tries just to take the bad along with the good, it all may seem irrelevant and, even worse, trivial, as life appears just to go round and round while we wonder what the gist of it is. One day I found a picture of myself as a small boy riding a merry-go-round. The photo probably was taken by my father, our seemingly omnipresent cameraman when we were growing up.

> From somewhere my picture was taken,
> tight smiling in hope I'll be found,
> riding for dear life a pony,
> as merrily we go round and round.
> Bigger ponies made me feel older,
> higher up the pole, up and down.
> My child, I've pushed to be up there,
> while merrily we go round and round.
> I climb on a horse yet more gilded,
> hurdy-gurdy churns out gay sound;
> then I would try something simpler,
> though merrily we go round and round.

Shooters Both

A number of poems have been written as people try to find some words or way to touch the mystery of life's ongoing suffering and where the caring of God's Spirit may be. Poets, too, are often keepers of the questions. The poet R. S. Thomas has written of George Herbert: "Yeats saw that out of his quarrel with others man makes rhetoric, but out of his quarrel with himself poetry. Herbert surely had no quarrel with others. What he had was an argument not with others, nor with himself primarily, but with God; and God always won." In Herbert's poetry one can often overhear a dialogue of the poet with self (of self with awareness) in which the divine Awareness is addressed and sometimes edges in. Herbert began his poem "Artillerie" with a startling image:

> As I one ev'ning sat before my cell,
> Me thought a star did shoot into my lap
> I rose and shook my clothes, as knowing well,
> That from small fires comes oft no small mishap.

The undertone of playfulness, which continues throughout the poem, begins in the absurdly calm manner with which the poet deals with such a fantastic event. He seems almost ready to ignore it. But then Herbert hears a voice speaking to him of his stubbornness and efforts to avoid engagement with God:

> I, who had heard of music in the spheres,
> But not of speech in stars, began to muse:
> But turning to my God, whose ministers
> The stars and all things are . . .

Earnest prayer, Herbert's contemporary John Donne more than once maintained, has about it the nature of impudence. We press God with a kind of "holy importunity" that God seems to allow if not encourage. In the spirit of this combat, Herbert realized that he had his own artillery with which he could return God's fire. His "shooters," his bursting shots and shooting stars, are, however, but his entreaties:

> But I have also stars and shooters too,
> Born where thy servants both artilleries use.
> My tears and prayers night and day do woo,
> And work up to thee; . . .

The prayer warfare seems so uneven, and, Herbert more than hints, greatly unfair:

> Not, but I am (I must say still)
> Much more obliged to do thy will
> Than thou to grant mine . . .

Yet, he persists, and so would God in this mock battle at once absurd and vital. The fight is fixed, but God invites it to continue:

> Then we are shooters both, and thou dost deign
> To enter combat with, and contest
> With thine own clay . . .

Herbert would like to come to some point of bargaining with God. "Let my arrows reach you and forget not my humanity," he asks.

> But I would parley fain:
> Shun not my arrows, and behold my breast.

One may again hear the voice of the psalmist similarly railing and pleading with God:

> I saw the prosperity of the wicked.
> . . . .
> They are not in trouble as others are;
>   they are not plagued like other people.
> . . . .
> When, at night, I cry out in your presence,
> . . . .
> For my soul is full of troubles,
>   and my life draws near to Sheol.
>   (Psalms 73:3–5, 88:1–3)

As an African American who knew the misery of plantation life put it, "You gotta shout and moan if you wants to be saved."

Yet "Artillerie" ends not unlike the Book of Job before Job's ultimate rewarding. There is no "articling" or bargaining with God. God remains

God; suffering and what often must seem to us to be evil and injustice go on.

When the Planes Crash

Herbert, Job, and the psalmist found, however, what they seemed most to be seeking. In the midst of life's tragedies and questions, they had prayed for some relationship with God's Spirit. Their plea for sense went unanswered, but their lamentations did find Presence. They were heard. I imagine this is what many others listen for in times of desperation. It was what I was most hoping for when I cried out as my plane careened out of control into Boston Harbor one frigid Saturday night in January. Some form of the prayer must be in nearly every heart when life goes out of control.

I was chaplain at Princeton when on that cold and rainy January evening, I boarded a flight for Boston. I was scheduled to preach the next morning at Harvard, but I had no idea quite how true to life that sermon would have to be.

By the time we arrived at Boston's Logan Airport, conditions had become much worse. The temperature was now below freezing. A sleety snow was falling, slanting off my Plexiglas porthole before racing away. The DC-10 seemed to land too fast and, for whatever reason, had trouble slowing. In the snowscape alongside the runway, I saw one, two, then three of the turnoffs hurtle by. I knew we were in big trouble.

There wasn't a sound on the plane. Either the other passengers did not realize what was happening or they had begun to clutch up as I had. I saw the last of the runway go, and there followed a series of sharp bumps. My prayer was short and primitive—that one-word petition, "Help!" Then I felt the plane swerve to the left, and I ducked my head. There was a much heavier bump, after which we seemed to go up in the air and then slam down. The top of my head banged hard into the seat in front of me.

After the crash, my first emotion was relief. My head smarted. I saw stars, but I did not seem to be injured. The plane had not exploded. I looked around. The rear engine was still roaring. I could hear yelling at the back of the plane. Other people were beginning to move around in the dim light. When someone said we were in the water, I looked out and saw dark waves lapping several feet below the window. It was then that we began putting on our life jackets.

There was no word from the captain or crew. It was another minute before we figured out that the force of the crash had sheared off the cockpit and tossed its crew into the harbor. Later we learned that the pilot's last words to the tower were "World 30 going over the end."

The blast of the engine in the rear made that exit impossible. People were surging toward the front. I couldn't take my carry-on luggage with me, but, in an impetuous moment that has amused other preachers, I reached into my briefcase, pulled out my notes for Sunday's sermon, and jammed them into my pocket. Maybe I was going to die, but if I didn't, I would have my sermon notes!

My seat was near one of the plane's front doors. With effort we were able to get it open, and the escape chute inflated into a great yellow slide. We floated the end of the chute over to the wing and, waddling down the wobbling slide, began to make our exit onto the slippery wing. I remember having the odd thought that this might even be fun on another occasion.

From the wingtip we had to wade only a few frigid yards to reach the shore. I looked back on the huge broken machine, once so powerful, now helpless in the water. The rear engine continued its wailing. It had sucked up the rear escape chute and spewed little bits of hot rubber over the plane and into some people's hair. The broken-off front section looked as if it had been severed from the rest by a giant cleaver.

I clambered over the rocks and up onto the runway, nearly falling several times on the icy tarmac. There was now a feeling of comradeship and pride among the passengers. We were alive, and there seemed to be few injuries. The plane had been full of young people returning from winter break to their college campuses. They probably were beginning to regard themselves as immortal again. Only later was that good feeling fractured by the news that a man and his elderly father had been thrown from the front of the plane and had drowned.

Only slowly, too, did we realize how lucky we all were. If the pilot had not swerved, we would have crashed into the landing bridge with its lights and high-tension wires. We were lucky the landing gear had broken off and that we had not gone out farther into the water.

But was it only luck, or was there more to our survival? I heard many complimentary references to God as we made our way safely to the terminal. Several people told me that they had joined me in one version or another of that foxhole prayer. And friends later assured me that God had rescued me and did not want me to die. *God had been my copilot.* Was that what I should say in my sermon in the morning?

But what should I say of the two that had died? What of the college president who survived the crash and died of a heart attack eight months later? What of all those who die in terror as other planes crash into oceans or hillsides or buildings?

Regardless of whether I could answer those questions, I could say that I had not felt wholly alone. No angel came to save, but I somehow felt not apart from a Presence that did know about me. Someone once sketched out for me the difference between what he called "Theology A" and "Theology B." Theology A goes like this: "If the children survive, if my doctor gives me a good report, if my business thrives, then I will give thanks and trust in God." Theology B, remembering Psalm 23, says, "Even though I walk through the valley of the shadow of death . . . you are with me."

❈

But can this be enough? After all his poignant anger, laced with accusations regarding the terrible Shoah of his Jewish people, even Elie Wiesel was able to pray, "I no longer ask You to resolve my questions, only to receive them and make them part of You." So we can keep the questions. We may even ask God to receive our questions, but, if we cannot have good without evil—if only a mixed world can exist, with inseparable beauty and evil, order and disorder, novelty and messiness, music and suffering, kindness and death all interleaved—why bother God? Why bother *with* God? A prophet was very bold when he spoke in the one God's name and proclaimed: "I form light and create darkness, / I make weal and create woe; / I the LORD do all these things. . . . I am the LORD and there is no other" (Isaiah 45:7,18). Truly, only God—and a great God at that—could be fully aware of and take responsibility for the woe and the darkness, as well as the good and the light, of the world. Evil and suffering would not, then, be attributed to some other god or force. In one way or another, evil and suffering are, along with the questions, part of God's story, too, while I still go on asking what difference could it make that such a God is always aware? What difference could it make that the plane crashes and the cancer grows and the cruelties happen in God's presence? After an Alaska Airlines plane with a broken tail section spiraled into the Pacific Ocean, I found myself, perhaps partly because of my own crash experience, helping to lead the service for the families and friends. I joined them in prayer and in hanging onto one another. But what more could be said?

And, then, there was the terror on the hijacked planes flown into the World Trade Center, the Pentagon, and the fields of Pennsylvania, followed by the thousands who died in the fires and the buildings' collapse. I was teaching in South Africa on September 11, 2001, having arrived in Durban the day before. At a little before four in the afternoon, the bishop of Natal said he had some terrible news: "Your country is on fire." I thought that an odd thing to say until, so far from home yet live on television, I saw the burning towers fall. My wife joined me, and our first and greatest fear was personal. We have a son who worked in the neighborhood of the World Trade Center. Miraculously we were able to get through to him late that night on the telephone. He was safe, although he had seen the second plane explode into the south tower. By then, however, we had learned that three of the hijacked planes were bearing people home to our home, Los Angeles. There, and in New York, Washington, and Boston in the weeks to come, were the bitter tears and mourning questions.

A few weeks later I stood, still almost disbelieving, on ground zero with the salvage workers and chaplains. The scrapyard of twisted metal with the burned-out buildings all around filled one's eyes. The dust from the still-smoldering ruins and the acrid stench seeped into the pores. One of the workers turned and observed how from these many hundreds of offices, rarely a piece of desk or chair or even a telephone remained—much less hands and faces. It was a graveyard—blood and bone turned to ashes. I couldn't stop thinking of those who leapt to their death rather than burn alive, of all the families devastated. Not only were suffering and death palpable, but also human brutality, evil, and the fires of vengeance. Here, too, is evil done in the name of God. In the aftermath of September 11, someone scrawled on a wall in Washington, "Dear God, save us from the people who believe in you." Seeing all this and feeling the other atrocities and apocalypses of our world, it is hard not to stare, like novelist Joseph Conrad's enigmatic character Kurtz, into the heart of darkness and mutter, "The horror, the horror." And standing there in that heart of horror, one already knew that the response would somehow have to be more horror and many more deaths.

Dying Daily

One Good Friday afternoon, I came across my sons Matthew and Stuart, at the age of nine or so at the time, in the backyard crucifying their G. I. Joe doll. They had him up on a stake and were spotting his hands, feet, and side with a red magic marker. I started to reprimand them but then caught myself. Of course, these priest's kids wondered what this crucifixion was all about. Thinking perhaps to engage them in theological discourse, I asked them whether they had any questions. But what they wanted to know was how long it had taken him to die and whether he had bled a lot. They did not ask me why he died or what this meant to God and us. But these questions, I knew, would come later.

In the early churches, some teachers were concerned about keeping the purity and uniqueness of God from being directly affected by the material world with all its wrongs and entropy. Divinity, they argued, could not have experienced suffering, and certainly not death, in Jesus. It soon became clear, however, that belief that the Spirit and Awareness of all life was present in the seeming God-forsakenness of the cross is at the heart of the Christian faith. Vital to Christian hope is the trust that God was present even as Jesus called out from the cross, "My God, my God, why have you forsaken me?" (Mark 15:34). A rescue party does not appear, but God, faith believes, was present in this contorted and disfigured bit of humanity, in the blood and agony of his abandoned death.

I remember once seeing a depiction of the Trinity—the three *persons* of the one God—with the great wings of the Spirit overarching the Father doubled over and gathering up the crucified Son. The agony and death were part of God's experience in a way at least similar to how our awareness may fully share in the suffering of one whom we love.

So portrayed, the cross thus became a sign that God is keenly aware of all crucifixions, knowing and feeling all that hurts and is wrong in a cross-shaped world. "If we believe that God is present in the God-forsakenness of the crucified Christ," maintains Jürgen Moltmann, "we see him everywhere." God continues to be present to a cruciform existence that seems to require suffering and wrong in order to be. God does not stand apart. There is no place, no time of tragedy for which God's Spirit is not the context and presence. God knows and feels. Whatever happens to us happens in God. Whatever happens to us happens to God. After Auschwitz, only a God who could be with a child on a terrible journey could in any sense be God—only a God who knows "dying daily."

"My heart did heave," George Herbert wrote, ruminating on all human grief:

> My heart did heave, and there came forth, O God!
> By that I knew that thou wast in the grief,
> To guide and govern it to my relief,
> Making a scepter of the rod:
> Hadst thou not had thy part,
> Surely the unruly sigh had broke my heart.
> . . . .
> Thy life on earth was grief, and thou art still
> Constant unto it, making it to be
> A point of honor now to grieve in me,
> And in thy members suffer ill.
> They who lament one cross,
> Thou dying daily, praise thee to thy loss.

Enlarging Compassion

Into the mystery of such compassion one may find invitation to join through awareness of others living in divine Awareness. Indeed, if one loves others, such empathy would seem unavoidable. It is in this Spirit that Jesus called those who would follow him to "deny themselves and take up their cross daily" (Luke 9:23). Rather than putting themselves first, they may participate in a love and service that demand compassion—a suffering with another. Love is that decision to let oneself be affected by another. "Anyone who loves," advises Moltmann, "dies many deaths."

In this way, too, humans with their spirits are invited to share in the sufferings of divine Awareness. People, noted the German martyr (sufferer/witness) Dietrich Bonhoeffer, who was put to death by Adolf Hitler, are often ready to go to God with their woes and needs:

> All go to God in their distress,
> Seek help and pray for happiness,
> Deliverance from pain, guilt and death.
> All do, Christians and others.

They may, he suggested, also share with the God of creation in the burden of all grieving. Hitler had Bonhoeffer hung naked in an attempt to strip him of any human dignity, but it brought his death even closer to that of Jesus:

> All go to God in his distress,
> Find him poor, reviled without shelter or bread,
> Watch him tormented by sin, weakness and death.
> Christians stand by God in his agony.

"It is not the religious act that makes the Christian," held Bonhoeffer, "but the participation in the suffering of God in the world."

Such compassion enlarges compassion. The more that is shared, the greater is the heart for this sharing. As suffering is allowed to enter in, new places in the heart come into existence. Or, as the elf Haldir suggests to Merry in *The Lord of the Rings*, "Though in all lands love is now mingled with grief, it grows perhaps the stronger." This growing and strengthening may well be at the heart of the universe. One can imagine the enlarging to be the secret to the ever-giving yet ever-living power of God—in which Awareness, human awareness, and compassion may share. Bonhoeffer's poem closes with this stanza:

> Consoling and reconciling God goes to all in their distress,
> Satisfies body and soul with his bread,
> Dies crucified for all Christians and others,
> And both alike forgiving.

The moving power of the offering anew of Jesus' last supper with his disciples is found in the significance of this dying and sharing recollected over and again at funerals and weddings, in thanksgiving and before an operation, in victory and defeat, in hope and sorrow.

Paul offered praise to "the Father of mercies and the God of all consolation, who consoles us in all our affliction, so that we may be able to console those who are in any affliction with the consolation with which we ourselves are consoled by God" (2 Corinthians 1:3–4). Sharing in suffering brings opportunities for sharing in consolation, both to receive and to offer consolation.

The God of all consolation may then be thought of as the Accompanier or Companion on the passage of life. The divine Awareness is the Companion-Sufferer who understands. Another analogy is with the parent who cannot always prevent or take away life's pain and suffering, but who loves the child and knows and shares in his or her hurt. This may be understood as God's way of honoring the human condition, in which, by compassion, the divine Awareness participates.

When pain and tragedy feel overwhelming, it may or may not seem that the companionship and compassion of God's Spirit are enough. But it is the story of faith that it is better than absence. It is the story of faith that this may be what, in their heart of hearts, people most want and hope for.

This would be the divine love, wiser than despair, seeking—perhaps reaching from a consummation beyond our time—to reconcile life to life. It is the understanding and compassion that can comfort and may bring healing and reconciliation. It is a beginning of the transformation of life's sorrows that may yet help us to say *yes* in the midst of all the tragedy and perplexity. In yet another plane crash, Dag Hammarskjöld, then the secretary-general of the United Nations, died while on a peacekeeping mission in Africa. Found in his home later was a kind of spiritual diary he had kept. In it he had written some very personal reflections—a dialogue with himself and then with the Spirit of life. Although he had known cause for despair, out of the struggle with discouragement, Hammarskjöld found that he finally could and wanted to say *yes* to life. *Yes*, it is still better that there be life and not only chaos. It is better to have this compromised world than for there to be no life and no awareness.

The achievement of this *yes*, I have come to believe, is aided by the Spirit, acting not on the world from without but, as it were, from the inside out—in and through human awareness. Friends and others may then become companions in reconciliation and caring. In this present life, in words attributed to Teresa of Ávila, "Christ has no body now on earth but yours, no hands but yours, no feet but yours; yours are the eyes through which is to look out Christ's compassion to the world; yours are the feet with which he is to go about doing good, and yours are the hands with which he is to bless us now." More than once, when called to be with Samiran's family or to share in some other death or tragedy, I have found my words and prayers clumsy and insufficient. Sometimes all one can do is to hold another person and shed tears as well. The first time this happened to me, I felt inadequate, but no longer does that bother me. The tears are the gift of one's empathy and presence, and I imagine them to offer something of the caring of God hidden in the suffering but otherwise powerless in the tragedy of the world.

In the context of divine Awareness, this acceptance and reconciliation come about by persuasion, not compulsion. Those whose awareness grows participate in the mystery that God seems to draw the world toward greater intensities of suffering. But part of this mystery is that to participate in the suffering means also to share in the forgiveness. It means to share in the empathy, the compassion, the healing, and the love, believing that only such love can make a difference. Only in this way may one stay in covenant with a God who stays in covenant with a suffering creation. Only in this way of God may we find heart to do all in the power of our awareness to offer mercy and compassion to others, to try to alleviate pain and bring about greater fairness of sharing, enabling reconciliation and inviting others also to participate in greater compassion and caring. In this way may we honor the divine Awareness and respond to God's love by adding to the ultimate consolation: the restoration and beauty of creation. In this way may we share in the divine imagination of all the love that can be. In this way may we share in the persistent faith of the seventeenth-century British poet Henry Vaughan: "And here in dust and dirt, O here / The lilies of his love appear!"

Another poet, John Keats, described our world as a "vale of soul-making." Philosopher of science Holmes Rolston III comments:

> Any elements of ordeal in nature have to be assessed against their contribution to soul making. Everywhere the ladder of ascent is climbed by problem solving. Nature produces a thesis, then an antithesis to it, and the result is a higher synthesis. Upward on the scale, joy and success come in counterpoint to agony and failure. The outcome is a dramatic quest for meaningful life.

Five ❀ While Knowing Ourselves

What I Do

The quest for a meaningful life! Wanting to lead a good life—a life of compassion that contributes to the lives of others and the human adventure—I tell myself this is what I hope for, what I most want. Surely many others do as well. Though life has its puzzles and can be bewildering, it offers many opportunities to be a caring and even a wise person. Perhaps, I ask, there are ways in which trying to live lovingly can bring one closer to a meaningful life than all the pondering and prayer. "Go and do likewise," Jesus tells the scribe who asks him about eternal life—that is, the life of lasting value (Luke 10:37). Offer compassion as did the Samaritan to the wounded traveler: "Do this, and you will live" (Luke 10:28). "Those who do not love a brother or sister whom they have seen, cannot love God whom they have not seen" (1 John 4:20). As the song's prayer goes, "Three things I pray; to see thee more clearly, to love thee more dearly, to follow thee more nearly, day by day." Maybe the last comes first. Trying to follow the way of love may be what draws one into the loving and seeing of the life of the Spirit. Right and generous living may, one can hope, lead toward life's more profound significance.

Essential to the quest would seem to be the enlargement of awareness so as to include others—to make place and space for them in life. By contrast, immature persons, we all quickly recognize, are people who do not have a developed awareness that takes significantly into account the hopes and needs of others. They do not *feel* for others. They think mostly of themselves, and, as someone once noted, people wrapped up in themselves make pretty small packages.

Why, then, while wanting to be a person that makes place for others, do I often end up being one of those small packages? What causes me to serve mostly or only myself and, even then, sometimes not very well? I remember how I both laughed and struck my forehead when I first paid attention to the Apostle Paul telling of this experience in his own inimitable fashion: "I do not understand my own actions . . . for I do not do the good I want, but the evil I do not want is what I do . . . wretched man that I am!" (Romans 7:15,19,24). *Why did I do that? Who am I really? I don't understand myself.* The self is here in dialogue with the self, almost as though two persons. In more classical psychological terms, this could be the superego (the critical part of the psyche, the enforcer of moral standards) and the id (the source of instinctual drives dominated by pleasure principles and irrational wishing) in contest (Paul's spirit and flesh). In the middle of this parliament of selves is a beleaguered ego, negotiating and trying to make some sense of it all.

The story of Adam and Eve, as we have seen, is another way of reflecting on the human condition. Maybe it would have been preferable for humans not to have attained the capacity to think upon thinking, to have come to see themselves as individuals and as actors, and to be able, among other things, to be self-critical. Certainly it might have been better not to know of mortality with all the fear and anxiety that result from that knowledge.

Some earlier interpreters blamed all our problems on this original sin of eating the forbidden fruit. One need not, however, even know the story of Adam and Eve to recognize that self-awareness can often seem like a pain and a burden. Wouldn't it be paradise not to be in dialogue with ourselves in this way?

Yet, referring to Adam and Eve's eating of the fruit, one of the hymns of the Easter vigil begins with the words, "O blessed iniquity." *Blessed sin.* Without self-awareness and its consequence—the ability to discern good from wrong and cruelty—and without some opportunity to choose, we could never be fully human and could never approach our potential.

Escape

Do we not often, though, want to forget about any potential for living beyond care for self? Frequently, I find, I would prefer to escape from the voice of my awareness. And, like Adam and Eve, who "hid themselves from the presence of the LORD God," I would just as soon avoid any divine Spirit in a relationship perhaps too mixed with my own voices to be sure what is what (Genesis 3:8).

Augustine, who, in his *Confessions* and other writings, had his own ways of keeping the questions, suggested that there are three results of human efforts to be forgetful and shut down their awareness. The first is illusion about the realities of life and what is of significance. There follows an inordinate desire for the things of the world that can help us achieve a state of distraction. And finally there is a weakness of will to do anything to change things. But who really wants to face up to this and be aware of all the possibilities and potential for a life lived beyond the self-focus of such illusion and desiring?

So, we have our strategies. Indeed, one can find perverse pleasure in commenting on other people's ways of coping, even while having to recognize one's own. Sleep is, of course, a necessary part of life. *Give it a rest!* is part of a rhythm we cannot do without. I once found a prayer attributed to Pope John XXIII and tacked it up on a wall where I can see it as I change into my pajamas: "There sure are a lot of problems in your Church, Lord. But they are your problems. You can handle it. I'm going to bed. Amen." Sleep is our balm and often a pleasure, but it can also become a kind of craving. In Robert Penn Warren's *All the King's Men*, Jack Burden is a former newspaperman who has lost his idealism in the service of a politician corrupted by his lust for power. Overwhelmed by his moral dilemmas, Jack "would come home in the evening, and because he knew that he could not work he would go to bed immediately. He would sleep twelve hours, fourteen hours, fifteen hours, feeling himself, while asleep, plunge deeper and deeper into sleep like a diver groping downward into dark water feeling for something which may be there and which would glitter if there were any light in the depth, but there isn't any light."

Along with sleep, sexual activity may seem a complex amalgam of the anticipation and warding off of death. Adam was asleep when his partner was made from his side, and it is no coincidence that sexuality has insinuated its way into the story in the Garden of Eden. However much pleasure sex offers, however much new life it may bring about, however much it draws one into a deeper relationship with another, part of the attraction of the tension and release of sexual orgasm lies in its capacity—at least for a few moments—to so self-absorb in sensation as to dull consciousness. Orgasm has, partly for this reason, been called "the little death"—a little like dying. From a biological perspective, it is interesting to recognize that in asexual reproduction, the parent cell divides and, in this sense, does not die, but goes on. Sexual reproduction, with its mixing of genes from different parents, proves to be a much better way of bringing about biological diversity and complexity. But the coming together of male and female also brings with it the requirement of parental death. These intimations of new life and death, joined with the forces that drive one to try to assert personal and genetic identity over others, are all a part of the fascination with sex. Then there are the resultant games of attraction, approval, rejection, and seduction that people may play, along now with whole industries that promote them as though these were the only games in town.

In my life and in the lives of many others, there is still so much to affirm and enjoy. Sexuality helps to make life stimulating, and the erotic imbues art and entertainment with élan and vitality. It lures people (sometimes of same-sex orientation) to one another and into intimate and vulnerable relationships that test the ability to care for another and to live with tenderness and forgiveness.

I remember once, when I was teaching undergraduates, I read a study that claimed that, at any given time in class, more than a quarter of college students are actually thinking about sex. The next day I looked about the lecture hall and tried to imagine that. And, of course, I was then thinking about sex too! Yet how can one avoid also observing manipulation and dominance, unwanted pregnancies, infections, adultery, and broken covenants? It is then hard not to be aware of how self-centered sexuality can be and how it can lead to a lot of foolishness, hurt, and even agony. One of the most painful parts of my professional life has been to deal with the sexual misconduct of clergy who, like too many legislators, presidents, teachers, doctors, and lawyers, abuse the power their positions can give them over others. Some of the otherwise smartest and cleverest men in the world have become fools—and sometimes not-so-kind fools—because of their sexual instincts and longing. Not least because of our anxieties about our own attractiveness, the whole subject can become highly self-absorbing and even turn into an obsession. The money that is made making use of sexual interest and arousal through movies, television, advertising, and the burgeoning pornography on the Internet is evidence of its power. When one also hears about all the sexual trade of young women, men, and children in our world, it is hard not to grow discouraged about aspects of human nature. It takes considerable maturity and care for others to recognize that what makes human sexuality different from the rest of the wholly instinctual animal world is the ability to deny sexual activity in order to use it selectively and, one hopes, with care for another. Only such a deepening awareness of the other can give the activity, sometimes called "making love," its full human significance.

And Other Coping Habits

Alcohol may seem to be a good escape, too, for a while. It dulls the mind and awareness. Or it may be drugs or prescription painkillers. Then there are people who can become so totally absorbed in their work that overwork squelches a greater self-awareness. Or it can be other forms of exertion or the diversion of dangerous activities. Even if we know these pursuits are not good for us, sometimes not good for our bodies and our relationships, it may be hard to resist their narcotic effects.

One does not wish unduly to magnify these coping habits, but one has to recognize that they can become, in a profound sense, the human condition. Even if it is not drugs, liquor, work, sex, or food, there may be some other search for habitual distraction in entertainments, shopping, or vacations to make time go by—to find ways of *killing* time. They become the self-serving habits woven into our personalities—keeping us from a more profound sense of personhood. The constant noise of music, movies, and talk radio is a way to keep the inner voice or voices at bay— muted or unheard. And then, of course, there may be loads of television. A more contemporary Jack Burden might come home and prop himself up in front of the tube before falling asleep. The *average* American now watches four hours of television a day—the equivalent of watching two months a year nonstop. Perhaps interactive time with the Internet may now more productively cut into television time, though this, too, may become an addiction.

Striving for notoriety and fame, gambling, playing the stock market, and purchasing and gathering things can also have habit-forming and narcotic effects. The accumulation of wealth is attractive because of the pleasures and security it offers, but above all because of the power it grants. In all the making, processing, leveraging with, and counting of money, it can be forgotten that money is spent to purchase, in one way or another, the labor, skills, and time of others. That is why money is power. We conveniently lose sight of how much it should remind us of our dependence on each other. Although I think I understand why we have a society where some person's financial reward is five or ten times more than another's, I find it difficult to appreciate why a relative few— even if they are smart and clever—should achieve rewards fifty or a hundred or a thousand times greater than those of others. What is one to think of a world economy in which the fifteen richest individuals are worth more than the gross national product of all sub-Saharan Africa? Recent financial scandals suggest that some executives and financial managers experience no end of human greed, rather than cultivating some sense of their roles of being in service to employees, clients, and stockholders.

"In the shadow of the hawk," observed Edna St. Vincent Millay, "we feather our nests." Would it not be better, I have often asked myself, to live in a more balanced society that shared a greater sense of common goods: the air, water, and beaches, but also energy resources, health care, education, and work opportunities? "The test of progress," Franklin Roosevelt once maintained, "is not whether we add to the abundance of those who have much; it is whether we provide enough for those who have too little." As a young man, I was inspired by those words. They may have been a form of political rhetoric, but I wanted to be part of such hope. Given various means of discrimination and the lack of medical care, education, sometimes work, decent housing, and even food for all too many people, could we not find more equitable ways to make available to all human beings the basis for a dignified life? Despite all our anxieties about not having enough for ourselves, is there not, in fact, with the application of sufficient ingenuity, enough to go around for such an *oikonomia*—an economy and community of living?

I sometimes laugh to think how I must have screwed up financially. I have known some of the richest people in the world. I have gone on fundraising trips with characters like Malcolm Forbes. I have also bumped up against a swindler or two. Two days before he was indicted for fraud (he was probably wearing a wire and recording our conversation), I was talking alone with Ivan Boesky, a man who wanted also to have his generous side. It was worth at least a smile, a few days afterward, to see how relieved my university was when Ivan rescinded his several-million-dollar pledge of support.

Among the well-to-do are college classmates, guys I knew back when and who have gone on to become highly successful venture capitalists, heads of major investment houses, CEOs of large airlines and defense contractors. Another classmate has made a several-billion-dollar mint using, in sophisticated ways, a fairly simple formula for buying into corporations and then forcing them to break up assets or otherwise taking, or more likely threatening to take, control before selling at a large profit. No doubt many others did very well. Classmates have had a variety of vocations and made many contributions to our common life, but I would have to guess that the median as well as the average assets of my classmates are, to say the least, considerably greater than my own.

Yet by almost any measure with regard to the rest of the world, I am rich—living economically in the upper one or two percent of the world's population. I could also try to boast in reverse about how much I love bargains, and say, with Henry David Thoreau, that the individual who is richest wants least. But that would be only partly true of me. I have to recognize as well that I have taken on lines of work where success is not measured in dollars, though even that observation now needs to be qualified for at least some clergy.

The bottom line, I have to ask myself, is how much have I tried to shape a society in which enough is provided for those who have too little? I can claim that I have made some efforts and that I have shared some of my money. Yet still I live with harsh poverty virtually next door while continuing to be strongly influenced, if not governed by, my anxieties—not just about having enough for self and family, but about not wanting to fall too far behind in obtaining the luxuries that others have.

Environmental Neglect

Then there is the evident inability to take well into account people of less means, those who will come after us, other creatures, and even enlightened self-interest when it comes to the natural world and our environment. I sometimes recall Blaise Pascal's rueful outpouring: "What a figment a human being is!! What a novelty! What a monster, what a chaos, what a subject of contradiction, what a prodigy! Judge of all things, foolish earthworm, trustee of truth, sinkhole of uncertainty and error, the glory and the rubbish of the universe." "Who," he continued, "will unravel this entanglement?"

We kid ourselves. *There is no definitive evidence*, we tell ourselves, *about the effects of species depletion or global warming.* And we destroy other species at such a rate that we will be leaving a biologically depleted world, not only for our children and grandchildren but for all the children that ever will be. We cross our fingers in the hope that technology will somehow fix things, all the while consuming as part of a society in which five percent of the population uses nearly thirty percent of its fossil fuel resources. Together we create a monumental portion of the world's garbage. Paper and packaging and forest are all expendable.

When polled, however, eighty percent of the voters in the United States say that environmental standards cannot be set too high. But such talk is evidently cheap. Only when gasoline and electricity become expensive do we even think of conserving them. Special interests quickly enter in. It is, we are told, the needs of the consumer-driven economy and keeping our American style of life that must come first. It is a matter of jobs and profit margins, or military security. And, truth be told, most of us are our own special interests when it comes to consumption. Politicians are understandably afraid to stand in the way. We cannot seem to help ourselves, and, as one cynic put it, expecting human beings to be environmentalists is like thinking goats can be gardeners. If nothing else, apathy takes its toll: *What difference can I make?*

How could it be different? In the first garden, Adam was told "to till it and keep it" (Genesis 2:15). The natural world has to be used for living, but the wise goal would be to use it without using it up. Maybe it is the bit of Native American in me and all the years I have canoed through the Ontario wilderness, but I so want to *keep* the wind and water clean, to *keep* the soil and other creatures well. I want to be sure there is space and place for others now and in the future. As individuals people can do numerous things, in neighborhoods, as faith communities, and in businesses. I do a few of them sometimes, but it takes a conversion truly to care. Much of the time I feel like one of those goats.

Turning In

But, I try to ask realistically, does not everybody want to feather their nest? Do not we all operate, at best, out of quite mixed and sometimes confused motives? The critical voices may seem just to come from an overactive conscience. *Give it a rest,* indeed! Some days I feel well prepared to join with those of generations past who, knowing that "our life will pass away like the traces of a cloud," offered this as their wisdom:

> Come, therefore, let us enjoy the good things that exist,
> and make use of the creation to the full as in youth.
> Let us take our fill of costly wines and perfumes,
> and let no flower of spring pass us by.
> Let us crown ourselves with rosebuds before they wither.
> Let none of us fail to share our revelry;
> everywhere let us leave signs of enjoyment,
> because this is our portion, and this our lot.
>
> (Wisdom of Solomon 2:6–9)

Perhaps, despite our poses, we are all locked into such a self-interest—all narcissists in one way or another. We can make ourselves attractive, even play the role of helper, but as the joke goes: "Enough about me. How about you? Tell me what you think of me."

Or maybe one could just settle for a gentle brand of stoicism and stop trying to see the human enterprise as such a grand opportunity to grow in awareness and empathy for others. With our complex brains and considerable consciousness, there are yet so many limitations and frailties, so many ways we are programmed by hundreds of generations of evolutionary psychology. And we have so many problems of our own to deal with. At least one might considerably lower expectations of what self-awareness can accomplish. *We're only human!*

I am, however, disappointed when I think this way—even brokenhearted over loss of hope with regard to a greater human goodness and love. Something in me did expect more—wants more. Martin Luther, probably more insightfully, described the natural human condition as *incurvatus in se*. We are turned inward on ourselves. In this he is following the Apostle Paul's insight that the human idea of freedom is to be able to do what we want when we want to do it, only to discover that we can only do what we want to do. Here they are both in agreement with a number of the sociobiologists. We may manage some enlightened self-interest and acts for the common good, but it is still the self wrapped up and trapped in the self, and so making up rather small packages. People can be nice enough when things are going reasonably well, but when push comes to shove, the masks come off. As the jingle puts it, "Even rich folks can be sinners when they don't get their dinners."

Where It Ends

The hardest part of accepting such self-centeredness is the loneliness that comes with it. Awareness, instead of being able to expand genuinely to include others, is ultimately ensnared within itself on its little would-be hedonic treadmill. That loneliness and subsequent melancholy are a major literary theme on what Tennessee Williams labeled "the mad pilgrimage of the flesh." Early in his play *Sweet Bird of Youth*, Williams's character Princess takes the loneliness a step further. After a night of seeking to dull and deaden her awareness, she manages to get up from the bed that dominates the stage. She looks out the window and sees the beach and some bathers "and then, an infinite stretch of nothing but water." She begins to sob. The young man who has spent the night with her asks, "What?" "Oh God," she responds, "I remember the thing I wanted not to. The goddam end of my life!"

Perhaps we should not see what we want not to see between four a.m. and the dawn, as Philip Larkin did:

> Till then I see what's really always there:
> Unresting death, a whole day nearer now,
> Making all thought impossible but how
> And where and when I shall myself die.
>
> The mind blanks at the glare . . . .
> . . . at the total emptiness for ever,
> The sure extinction that we travel to
> And shall be lost in always, Not to be here
> Not to be anywhere . . . .
>
> And so it stays just on the edge of vision,
> A small unfocused blur, a standing chill
> That slows each impulse down to indecision.

If a number of philosophers and psychologists are right, most of us spend a good deal of our time trying to keep the blur unfocused. We want to deny that for us, as was true before we were born, there will be nonbeing. We are made, as the psalmist would have it, "a little lower than God, / and crowned with . . . glory and honor" (Psalm 8:5). Yet we "are like the animals that perish" (49:12). "Their days are like grass; / they flourish like a flower of the field; / for the wind passes over it, and it is gone, / and its place knows it no more" (Psalm 103:15–16). "Remember that you are dust, and to dust you shall return," I hear in the church's Ash Wednesday service, as though I needed reminding. No matter! For, as Larkin concludes, "Death is no different whined at than withstood."

Death is never tamed, but because we cannot keep thinking about it, the anxiety has gone, as it were, underground. From there, in tension with efforts at repression, come inner forces that can be destructive through our coping addictions. (One can understand why people of earlier times felt such forces to be like demons within.) From there also issues the creative energy that fuels a good deal of artistry. From Homer to Hemingway, much art may well be born in a form of pain—at least in a deep longing to fashion something—a painting, a story, a song, what I now write—that will for a time offer the illusion of staying the seepage of time and will last beyond the death lurking in us. Many of the greatest artists seem to have experienced great pain over life's many losses and the prospect of death. This may be a major reason their work speaks to others, offers sympathy, and can be piercingly beautiful. Ironically, that same beauty may occasion the reverse emotions of resentment and even anger that what is fashioned is going to outlive the artist: *Life is short; art is long.* Yet even art is not forever. In spite of all our technological advances and storage techniques, what we write and create is being lost at a faster and faster pace.

Would that we could—even for a long moment—hold still the passage of time. Would that we were able to leave some scratch of our initials on the rock of eternity. I wrote my college senior thesis on the strategies of the novels of Virginia Woolf, who late in life committed suicide by putting a stone in her pocket and walking into the river Ouse. She has her characters, who are sometimes artists themselves, yearn to "hold the scene—so—in a vice and let nothing come in and spoil it." They long to master the time that would otherwise master them. In *To the Lighthouse*, the novice painter Lily remembers "Mrs. Ramsey saying, 'Life stand still here'; Mrs. Ramsey making of the moment something permanent. . . . In the midst of chaos there was shape; this eternal passing and flowing (she looked at the clouds going and the leaves shaking) was struck into stability."

But the ever-rolling stream moves on. Although it is a current in which all share, we may yet find ourselves made more lonely and, with Princess, pressed further into our coping selves.

Captains of Morality

Religion has a mixed record in helping people reach out in care beyond themselves. Probably most people want to see themselves as moral and ethical. They want to believe themselves good or at least justified in their actions. Unfortunately the apparently easiest way to do this is to put down or exclude others as inferior. Whole classes or even ethnic groups may be dealt with in this way, but the activity can also focus on individuals. Such putting down is a major function of gossip. One notes how gossipy politics is, and, I suppose, it is as true among bankers, lawyers, teachers, poets, ballplayers, clergy, and movie stars. People can be hard on one another without the benefit of religion, but religious morality, because its codes of conduct may be seen to come from beyond human laws and mores, can have a strongly reinforcing effect. Faith's adherents want to see themselves on the side of rightness, sometimes at the expense of others.

Two men go up to the temple to pray. One, in Jesus' story, is a Pharisee (a member of a devout religious group) and the other a tax collector (see Luke 18:10–14). The Pharisee, standing apart, prays: "God, I thank you that I am not like other people: thieves, rogues, adulterers, or even like this tax collector. I fast twice a week; I give a tenth of all my income." The tax collector, standing far off, won't even look up to heaven. He beats his breast and says, "God, be merciful to me, a sinner." Jesus declares the tax collector, and not the Pharisee, to be the man who went home justified.

But, one may ask, what is wrong with this Pharisee? He was

evidently a right-living person. Pharisees at the time gave more than ten percent of their livelihoods for religious and charitable purposes. They fasted twice a week. One may think he is self-righteous, but he does thank God for his condition, and, in their time, Pharisees were known for their humility. In the story, however, the Pharisee is seen as seeking to establish his own goodness on the back of the tax collector, causing him to stand far off, away from the "acceptable members" of the religious community. The Pharisee needed someone to compare himself with so that he could see himself as more upright.

Often one detects insecurity in the putting down of others. *Maybe he's a good scholar, but he's not a very good teacher.* If we can't question accomplishments, we can always wonder out loud about motives. *Perhaps she's an important person, but she got there only because she is so ambitious. She certainly knows how to step on others.* People can try to establish who is *in* as far as rightness is concerned by defining who is *outside* the circle of acceptable behavior. An ethical competition develops as people struggle to establish their worth in their own eyes. In overt or subtle ways, few people have not at one time or another felt the frowning glance, like that coming from the Pharisee or from some other captain of morality.

The religious effort to know or prove that one has worth can take subtle forms. Historically one of the more convoluted of these begins by trying to show that no one can boast of goodness because no one is worthy of acceptance as righteous by God. Only by God's grace are some chosen for salvation. Others are not so chosen. No human deserving or status is involved in this. The only way, then, of knowing whether one has been made okay with God is by signs of living a righteous life by God's grace. One only knows one is good by being good. Now comes the problem. If one is not wholly good and commits sins, then there will have to be questions as to whether one is really saved and on the side of righteousness. To do battle with the possibility that one is not saved requires more than the hypocritical effort of trying to hide sinfulness from others or disguise it. One needs to find ways to deal with the cognitive dissonance (one's beliefs and actions not matching up) by disguising wrongdoing from oneself. A lot of what politicians call "spinning" and Huck Finn called "stretchers" has to go on. One must not admit that one is acting from anything other than right motives—the motives of a person or, for that matter, a whole nation—made righteous. To fully understand United States foreign policy through the past two and a half centuries, it is helpful to recognize the influences on a number of its architects of the sense of being a chosen people with a manifest destiny. It was and remains hard for many Americans to recognize, much less admit, the mixed motives in the nation's political, economic, and military strategies and actions.

One would like to think that there are heroes of religious faith who rise above any such self-serving motives, at least the Albert Schweitzers and the Mother Teresas. It's hard to know. I once heard an archbishop of Canterbury puckishly refer to some of the better-known saints as "conspicuous Christians whose lives have been insufficiently researched." In this view, such saints may have done much good, but they were also men and women with neuroses and whose energy for living sometimes seemed to come from odd places. And, I ask, does this, too, fall in the category of gossip? Do I, at least for the moment, feel better for having made this observation?

The Good Problem

Is it, then, impossible to transcend self-interest and at least begin to care for another and others as oneself? The sociobiologist might grant that a person could have a measure of what at least feels like such care for those close to us who meet our needs and for members of the closely related gene pool—our clan. This still, however, is in many ways a self-serving care. Granted the beauties of family love, such care is still dictated by a concern with self-preservation and the continuation and aggrandizement of a particular gene pool. The family becomes the selfish unit and the excuse for being self-serving.

Yet, if self-interest can be enlarged for the sake of one's family, might the golden rule of "Do to others as you would have them do to you" then be further extended to take into consideration a larger group—the neighborhood and still larger community—in efforts to establish certain common goods that may be shared? One may even be ready to qualify certain self-interests by, for instance, willingly paying taxes or making donations for a hospital or a park from which many people can benefit. The equations can become more complex if one's donations are rewarded with a name on a building or a plaque in the lobby. But, still, a larger self-interest has been forged, and whole philosophies of ethics and theories of government are based on such enlightened interest. They are based on explicit and implicit contracts of cooperation with a view to the goods of common living that can result. At their best, any number of human accomplishments flow from such contracts and standards of behavior: schools, volunteer fire departments, libraries and gardens, houses of faith, cooperative stores, businesses, and other enterprises. One can recognize the reciprocities involved and the games of self-interest that are being played, but the whole human enterprise would be vastly diminished without them.

What is learned from evolution and forms of social Darwinism is sometimes used to suggest an unending evolutionary arms race in which there must always be winners and losers. The popular *Survivor* television program and its clones can take this ideology to the extreme of the lone survivor. In real life, however, lone survivors soon die. Life cannot go forward without many symbiotic and cooperative relationships. A developed human self-interest and awareness understand well the significance and value of many forms of mutual assistance.

One can, however, also see so much that goes wrong when people begin to cheat on the game or contract or otherwise not contribute or do what is seen as their fair share. After a year or two, the communal picnic may be abandoned if even a small group regularly shows up with appetites but no food to share. (Children notice the problem with other kids right away: "Hey, they're not sharing!") On a much larger scale, care for the environment crumbles when the majority say, in effect, *You others have to improve your policies first or we won't improve ours.* In all too many human circumstances, there is strife-filled competition or, in worst-case scenarios, people go to war over what are seen as limited resources.

In the large perspective, we may have to console ourselves and recognize that such losses are the prices that have to be paid in the complex game of life. Yet, in the same passage in which Jesus presents the golden rule, he continues:

> If you love those who love you, what credit is that to you? For even sinners love those who love them. If you do good to those who do good to you, what credit is that to you? For even sinners do the same. If you lend to those from whom you hope to receive, what credit is that to you? Even sinners lend to sinners, to receive as much again. But love your enemies, do good, and lend, expecting nothing in return. Your reward will be great, and you will be children of the Most High; for [God] is kind to the ungrateful and the wicked. Be merciful, just as your Father is merciful. (Luke 6:32–36)

Clearly the stakes have been raised considerably. There is yet reciprocity for this extraordinary behavior in that disciples are said to receive a reward. But the reward is found in emulating the character and ways of God based on the analogy of a child learning from a parent. Followers of Jesus are to try to love their enemies and to be merciful because these are the characteristics of God.

As I read the passage again, I do not know whether to laugh or cry. I may laugh because it seems so impossible to live by this teaching. I can smile when I think how, from a sociobiologist's point of view, the passage could be heard as another sophisticated gambit in the game of trying to get others to cooperate in living together without too much contention and strife. Everyone could benefit. Sooner or later, however, it is bound to break down. It has, for this reason, been called an interim ethic—one that can at best be approximated only during the interim when God's ultimate realm or ruling way is presumed to be about to establish itself. When that end does not come, the ethic must end too.

And, so, I may weep too. Would that human beings might live by these ways and have a love of neighbor as oneself that included self but, in some self-transcending measure, genuinely included others as well. Perhaps the most profound manner of reciprocity could be discerned in this. Perhaps one imagines a far better humanity emerging for all. Would that it were not so impossible!

Or might there be yet another response? Could one at least still aspire to live this more open and vulnerable way with others? Yes, there is the problem of evil—the problem of so much selfishness and suffering in the world. But why is there not only that selfishness? There is at least this aspiration to take the needs and sufferings of others more fully into account and to treasure stories of human love and nobility that seem to do so. There are the stories of Jesus coming "not to be served but to serve"; of a mother's love for another mother's children; of firefighters at the World Trade Center; of a holocaust survivor nourishing a starving Nazi soldier back to life; of forgiveness and reconciliation after the brutalities of apartheid in South Africa. The mere possibility of this aspiration grips and captures the human heart, even if only on our best days. Why? Why would we even imagine that this goodness could be a part of the human adventure? How does one account for this "good that I would do"—the spirit of extraordinary generosity and self-giving that continues to inspire?

"If I am not for myself, who will be? But, if I am only for myself, who am I?" It would not make much sense not to care for oneself. One cannot care for others unless one cares for oneself. But what *good* would life be if one could not care for others? These words of wisdom from a rabbi of long ago describe a rhythm for life. One cannot care for others without self-care, but when one also at least begins to love the neighbor as oneself, a larger vision for life shines. From within the often fearful, guarded, habitually coping ego, what John Donne called "the abler self," the larger self with an awareness of self and others, begins again to venture out and live in empathy and with the wisdom that comes from a greater understanding of others.

The Healing

There are days when I am so unsure. Whatever we want to believe, natural instincts may not allow such an abler self to emerge and transcend ego in the interest of profound empathy and compassion. I do know from my experience of my own insecurities and fears that this tentative emerging and risking cannot take place without knowing love and acceptance. I cannot care well for others until I become well by love—made able to love by being loved and valued.

This love may come from others. At its best it is a forgiving love, accepting us with our faults, even if, as with a mother's love, the acceptance continues to hope for the best from us. Some years ago there was a youngster who lived down the block from our home. He frequently had a dirty face and a runny nose. He also had a precociously sarcastic mouth. Once I had to chide him for kicking gravel from our driveway onto the lawn. Another time I saw him push a little girl off her tricycle.

Sometime later the lad's parent invited my wife and me for dinner. As we were sitting in the living room with our drinks and snacks, this boy came downstairs in his blue and white pajamas, fresh from his bath. He sat on his mother's lap and she ran her fingers through his shining hair.

That may seem like an easy one, but Jesus told a not-dissimilar story about a wastrel prodigal son and the love of a parent who seemed almost unable to contain himself when it came to accepting his children (see Luke 15:11–32). The young man had foolishly and selfishly wasted his share of his father's living. But now the son had come home! The father welcomed him with gifts of clothes, a ring, and sandals, and a party with the prized fatted calf as the centerpiece. The same father then went out into the fields to try to convince his hardworking elder son ("All these years," complained the son, "I have been working like a slave for you.") that he should come and join the party. "You are always with me, and all that is mine is yours," responded the father. Jesus evidently prayed to God as such an *Abba*, as a parent to both his prodigal and his self-righteous children.

Zacchaeus was a still tougher case. Short of stature and a chief tax collector, Zacchaeus was probably at once greedy, insecure, and in the pay of the occupying Romans while yet wanting to be regarded as a good and important man (see Luke 19:1–10). Doubtless many in the crowded streets of Jericho on the day Jesus was passing through thought that he would want to stay and share a meal with several of the actually right-living folk in town. The anticipated religious message, after all, remains *Be good, behave, and then God might accept you.* Yet, even before Zacchaeus was able to get to a promise to amend his life, Jesus called him down from the tree he had climbed to see over the heads of the crowd. "Zacchaeus, hurry and come down; for I must stay at your house today."

I hear such stories and hope is again awakened. I want to believe that I am accepted like that by one who knows all my "stuff," all my pretenses and coping habits, and my love—at least my desire to love. "For God," hoped also the author of *The Cloud of Unknowing*, "with the all merciful eyes sees not what you are or have been, but what you would be."

Made able to love by being lovable! I think the prodigal son and Zacchaeus may have been in the mind of George Herbert when he wrote a poem with allusions to several stories woven together. A dusty traveler is graciously welcomed. At another level the poem is a rite of courtly and courteous love (*sweetly questioning, smiling, my dear, took my hand, Love*). The poem Herbert called "Love" is, as well, a story of the soul and its Lord with overtones of Holy Communion and Jesus' giving of himself in the meal.

Love bade me welcome: yet my soul drew back,
    Guilty of dust and sin.
But quick-ey'd Love, observing me grow slack
    From my first entrance in,
Drew nearer to me, sweetly questioning,
    If I lack'd anything.
A guest, I answer'd, worthy to be here:
    Love said, You shall be he.
I the unkind, ungrateful? Ah my dear,
    I cannot look on thee.
Love took my hand, and smiling did reply,
    Who made the eyes but I?
Truth Lord, but I have marr'd them: let my shame
    Go where it doth deserve.
And know you not, says Love, who bore the blame?

My dear, then I will serve.
You must sit down, says Love, and taste my meat:
So I did sit and eat.

The traveler, the soul, the beloved, the poet, and the hearer of the poem find that, despite all the protestations of unworthiness, and a final attempt to gain some control of the situation by taking the role of the server, such gracious acceptance cannot be merited. This welcoming and yearning love is a gift, as love and friendship always are, and the poem, full of intricate emotion, comes to its resolution in monosyllables—more passionate for their simplicity.

I sit and begin to eat. I, too, taste this love. The meat given for me warms and strengthens my heart. I look up and around. There is food and place at the table for others—a space opening to be a safe dwelling with God and friends. Together we are aware of our sometimes desperate human fragility and hunger, finding forgiveness and beauty at meal together.

The Gem

When Bob Dylan sang "In this age of fiberglass I'm looking for a gem," one wonders if he might have been imagining some similar spaciousness opening out. Perhaps, too, he recalled Jesus' analogy of the merchant looking for beautiful pearls. One day the merchant found one more precious than all others. He sold all he had and bought it—what was of surpassing worth. I think C. S. Lewis had it right, however, when he realized that our greatest hope is not satisfied in seeing or somehow possessing beauty. We want to share in it. We want to become part of the beauty, a part of this generous space with others, and to share in the divine empathy and compassion. From the lore of several cultures, one finds other stories about a gem along these same lines.

One learns of a traveler who asked an old man he met in the woods for directions and a little food. When the man opened his basket to offer him some of his bread, the traveler spied a jewel that he realized had to be of great worth. The old man explained that he had recently found it, and the traveler made bold to ask if he could have the beautiful stone. To his surprise and delight, the man readily agreed, and the traveler headed for home overjoyed. The wealth of the jewel would bring him great pleasures and security. But only a few days later, the traveler came back searching for the old man. Returning the gem, he asked if he could now have something he realized was far more precious. "Share with me what enabled you to give it to me."

A seeker asked Jesus, "What must I do to inherit eternal life?" The *life* he was asking about is not life that just goes on and on, but living that truly matters. Jesus lets the scribe answer his own question. Such life, he responds, is found in loving God with all one's heart and soul, strength and mind, and in loving one's neighbor as oneself.

But it is easy to recite those traditional words. How, this lawyer wants to know, does one manage to do this amid the exigencies and demands of everyday living? One cannot be loving to everyone. "Who is my neighbor?" "Who," he really is asking, "is *not* my neighbor?"

As he so often does, Jesus responds with a story—in this case, a story about a man who, traveling down the road from Jerusalem to Jericho, falls into the hands of robbers. They strip him and beat him and run away, leaving him half dead. A priest sees him and passes him by. Then a Levite (a lay religious leader) sees him and passes him by. The next to come by is a traveling Samaritan, who is moved with pity. He stops and leans down and bandages his wounds, having poured oil and wine on them. He then puts him on his own animal, brings him to an inn, and takes care of him. The following day he gives two denarii to the innkeeper and says, "Take care of him; and when I come back, I will repay you whatever more you spend" (Luke 10:30–35).

The remarkable heart of this story is the help offered by one person to another even though the Samaritan did not need to do this and expected nothing in return. A Samaritan traveling in Judea could easily have said, "This wounded man is no brother—no kindred of mine." Instead, he stops and, despite danger and certainly inconvenience to himself, offers extraordinary care and generosity.

The main figure in the story, the person with whom all others come in contact, is not the Samaritan but the injured man. The lawyer who asked the question about eternal life is asked to experience the surprise and gratitude of the lonely and desperate man helped by someone who could so easily have passed him by. The Samaritan did not need to ask, "Who is my neighbor?" Could the scribe find the love and sympathy to live like that?

"There is no greater sign of holiness than the procuring and rejoicing in another's good," attests George Herbert. Those who want only to save their life, Jesus said, will lose it. "All is lost unless it is given," is the wisdom of an ancient eastern proverb. The beauty of the gem is known in sharing it with others. Nothing else matters like this. "If," as Paul came to believe, "I give away all my possessions, and if I hand over my body so that I may boast, but do not have love, I gain nothing. Love is patient; love is kind; love is not envious or boastful or arrogant or rude. It does not insist on its own way" (1 Corinthians 13:3–5). Such love may seem to be only the ideal of love—the ideal of God's way of loving, but not ours. Yet there is the calling to follow in this way. One may at least aspire to begin to live with and in such beauty—to live as if love is the heart of all that matters. Can I begin to live and love like that?

Six ⁂ While Restless and Resting

Still Searching

Amid such intimations of beauty and the adventure of life's opportunities for friendship and compassion, I find myself yet searching. Many of us are. There remains a longing—for what, we are not sure. This longing and reflection are themes of much prayer and religious reflection, and of art and literature more generally. The first of the Four Noble Truths of Buddhism is *dukkha*, life is suffering, which often results from a state of feeling unsatisfied. One's greatest success—whether it is professional, financial, writing a new poem, or having a fabulous relationship—may yet leave one feeling that something is missing. The experience of this lacuna can be disturbing. Despite all life's pleasures and pageantry, there is yet a sense of being unfulfilled, of being disappointed in small as well as more significant ways. The desires that ignite passion at the same time undermine our certainty. The human mind with its awareness has so much curiosity and sense of potential. In the context of mortality and with all life's limitations, there continues a searching—wishing for what we struggle to name. Perhaps this is in large part because all seems to pass away. More than one commentator has made the unsettling observation that evolution seems to have played a rather nasty trick by bringing into existence human beings vast in their desire and potential but minute in fulfillment and satisfaction.

In his poem "The Pulley," George Herbert surmised that God made humanity this way, with a discontent and restlessness that will never be satisfied with the beauty, honors, and pleasures of life. No achievement can fully satisfy. It may only awaken hunger for something more.

> When God at first made man,
> Having a glass of blessings standing by;
> Let us (said he) pour on him all we can:
>
> So strength first made a way;
> Then beauty flow'd, then wisdom, honor, pleasure:
> When almost all was out, God made a stay,
> Perceiving that alone of all his treasure
> Rest in the bottom lay.

God hopes, suggested Herbert, that the desire for fulfillment of our truer and *abler* selves will be the lure. The discontent and longing, in other words, are essential to full humanity. The search for the fullness of peace in reconciliation, caring, and community will draw us toward relationship with God. If that does not work, maybe a certain weariness with the transitory pleasures of life will do the job.

> Yet let him keep the rest,
> But keep them with repining restlessness:
> Let him be rich and weary, that at least,
> If goodness lead him not, yet weariness
> May toss him to my breast.

Time and again the psalmist expressed this longing:

> As a deer longs for flowing streams,
> So my soul longs for you, O God.
>
> (Psalm 42:1)

My soul longs, indeed it faints
for the courts of the Lord.

(Psalm 84:2)

O God, you are my God, I seek you.
my soul thirsts for you;
my flesh faints for you,
As in a dry and dreary land where there is no water.

(Psalm 63:1)

Prayer becomes the longing of the soul. "The heart is restless," Augustine knew, "until it rests *ad te*—toward (or, in relation with) you." God, in words of John Donne, is "the God of security, and the enemy of security too." "Your will," Dante believed, "is our peace." I want at least to begin to experience the resting of that peace.

Look Busy!

There is, however, in many of our cultures a prejudice against any such resting. I know it within me. I want to be building—to take on the opportunities to offer compassion, while, I suppose, building a reputation for doing so. There are books like this one to be written, programs, buildings, and institutions to be built and built up. And all along there are the voices, including even the Church's prayer of confession that regularly reminds us that we have "left undone those things which we ought to have done." When, as the joke goes, the assistant races breathlessly in to the head pastor's office with the news that "Jesus is coming!" and asks, "What should we do?" the response is: "Look busy, man! Look busy!"

Whether we think Jesus is coming or not, and whether or not religious faith provides the motivation, the work ethic is still strong. Worth comes from working and doing. It becomes a status symbol (as well as a way of warding off the requests of others) to be overly busy. Recently I tried a little experiment on a student who came to me. "Excuse me, she began tentatively, "I know you're terribly busy." "No, I'm not," I responded, and she didn't know what to say next.

But most of the time, we do think of ourselves as busy. The choices in life seem to keep proliferating from, for example, the myriad ways of counting carbs and calories to the almost infinite number of options on the new cell phones and then modes of combining them within the various plans for minutes and monthly charges. Multitasking becomes a necessity. With e-mail, pagers, and cell phones, one need never be out of touch. Microprocessors have continued to double in power and halve in size every two years, while nanotechnology may soon make present information overloads look like child's play. Even now the results from search engines can cause the eyes to glaze over. If there is a lull in the information rampage, it can quickly fill up with talk-radio, TV, and background music. And it is myself I see pressing the buttons and mouse, turning the knobs, and standing there with the TV remote in my hand, cycling through the channels and complaining that there is nothing on.

In the midst of all the hurry-worry, we may find ourselves frustrated by all the waiting and what seems like a waste of our time. We may be in a hurry, but we wait in traffic, at the tollbooth, and at the checkout counter. Then off we go to the airport: We wait to have our bags inspected, to check in, to get our boarding pass. There is the security line, and then the wait because we did get there early, followed by the line to give up the boarding pass, the backup in the jetway and then in the aisle to get a coat stowed away, and finally we sit and wait for some air traffic delay. Later we wait to land and wait for our baggage, and hope it is there. I have flown across the country in a few hours, but still seem to have spent much of my day hurrying and waiting.

Action in Inaction

One tries to gain perspective. Waiting need not be wasting. There can be attentiveness to a greater awareness of self and the world about while seeing and breathing and listening and praying. I think of the bird-watcher. Or on a misty Canadian morning, I wait to see a moose with her little one. One can learn the significance of patient waiting, listening, attentiveness, and quiet. In a drawing class, I am told, ten percent is drawing and ninety percent is seeing. The poet, too, is first attentive. The eyes and ears of appreciation and compassion can take time. This *attending* can shape expectation and alertness. It can offer a seeing and hearing of what otherwise might be missed in life. An attentive patience and greater awareness of what is significant and what is worth waiting for can form.

Simone Weil, a believing, attentive quester who never felt called to join the Church, noted all the waiting in the Bible. She saw the virtue in persevering longing—even in affliction. It was a way of faithfully keeping the questions. There is waiting for children, for escape from slavery, for the promised land, for the prophet, for return from exile, for rebuilding the city and temple, for wisdom, for the messiah, for the reign of God, for God's presence. Often the gift when it comes might easily be missed—a meal together, a still small voice, a seed, a baby.

Then there is life waiting: for the holidays, for a birthday, to grow up, for a career, for love, perhaps to be married, for children, for success, to be wiser, to be mature, to retire, for a diagnosis, for the meaning and value of life. Prayerful waiting can sharpen vision and be a way of being and becoming.

Over and again the psalmist's soul "waits for the Lord," more eagerly even than those who await the dawn—"more than those who watch for the morning, / more than those who watch for the morning" (130:6). "Wait for the LORD; / be strong, and let your heart take courage; / wait for the LORD!" (27:14). "Be still before the LORD, and wait patiently" (37:7). Prayerfulness may be thought of as hope-filled attention to the compassion and goodness of God. Attentive waiting is a form of devotion. In this context and perspective, one may better see what are the needs and goods for others along with self. There can be a quieting and healing of fear, anxiety's greeds, and jealousy's competitiveness. With a greater awareness of self in this larger context of divine Awareness, there may be an accompanying letting go of ego and a nonanxiousness that can then be brought to living. The "abler self" may grow.

Meister Eckhart speaks of the apparent paradox of "action through inaction." One thinks again of the bird-watcher disciplined for patient waiting and keen observation. Sometimes considerable effort is required to remain this still and attentive. Outside my window I see a hummingbird whirring hundreds of times a minute on pinion wings so that its steady bill can draw nectar from a flower. A swift alertness can have this purpose in the flux of life, suggested Robert Frost:

> And you were given this swiftness, not for haste
> Nor chiefly that you may go where you will,
> But in the rush of everything to waste,
> That you may have the power of standing still.

When in the Bhagavad-Gita, Lord Krishna urges Arjuna to take the action of meditation, he says, "One who sees inaction in action and action in inaction has understanding and is disciplined in all action he performs."

The French have a saying: *Reculer pour mieux sauter. Reculer* means "to draw back," even "to delay, postpone." *Sauter* is "to leap, to jump, to spring." One draws back in order to get a better look and to draw strength to leap. The drawing back is a kind of action in inaction, while the resulting action will have with it an alertness and awareness that might otherwise have been missing.

Yet the drawing back and resting, I have learned, need not be seen as only for the purpose of better jumping. The resting of the sabbath day—the human response to the story of God resting on the seventh day after the six days of creation—is meant for appreciation, attentiveness to beauty, and listening. There should be time in life to hear the stories of others—their hopes and fears, their worries and joys and longings. Resting is also for relationship—not least a relationship that calls us beyond ourselves into greater awareness and Awareness.

Gentle Consent

The resting can be easy. All that seems necessary is the consent to being there. Even amid all life's busyness, one can rest in the context of Awareness. And yet, as with any form of relationship, the resting may be hard to maintain. One's consent can equivocate. It may especially do so if one seems invited to share more of one's own spirit and selfhood. One's guard may again begin to go up as separateness feels endangered. Not infrequently during times of reflective meditation, I have heard my inclination chiding, *This isn't going anywhere*. Later it may seem that, in fact, I was discovering again just how guarded I can be about the separateness of my awareness. I recall, too, Screwtape's devilish advice to his assistant Wormwood in C. S. Lewis's *The Screwtape Letters*. When individuals begin to spend more time at prayer, Screwtape advised, it can be very useful to encourage them to analyze the value of their time at prayer. They should be counseled to take their temperature, as it were, with regard to the warmth of their feelings and the progress they are making. Soon they will be concentrating on their needs and feelings rather than being in relationship.

One realizes again that all the goodness and value of the consent to rest in relationship cannot be readily assayed or comprehended. That is true of any relationship of sharing with another and discovering a greater awareness of self and other. It may be especially so in relationship with the Spirit of all life. Wendell Berry counsels:

> The mind that comes to rest is tended
> In ways that it cannot intend.
> Is borne, preserved and comprehended
> By what it cannot comprehend.

Knowing is limited to what can be comprehended. Thomas Aquinas taught that the process of knowing involves taking information into the mind and is, therefore, limited to its own capacities. Relationship, on the other hand, expands the self's awareness. It takes the self beyond self, and, when the relationship is loving, further opens and enlarges. "Only to our intellect is God incomprehensible," taught the author of *The Cloud of Unknowing*, "not to our love."

Thus time and again men and women of prayer experience struggle in their effort to consent to be in the larger context. All manner of other thought and distraction may occur, and it ceases to be resting. More than three hundred years ago, John Donne described this condition for every fidgety self:

I throw myself down in my chamber, and I call in and invite God and his angels thither and when they are there, I neglect God and his angels for the noise of a fly, for the rattling of a coach, for the whining of a door. I talk on, in the same posture of praying; eyes lifted up; knees bowed down, as though I prayed to God; and if God or his angels should ask me when I last thought of God in that prayer, I cannot tell. Sometimes I find I had forgot what I was about, or when I began to forget it, I cannot tell. A memory of yesterday's pleasures, a fear of tomorrow's dangers, a straw under my knee, an anything, a nothing, a fancy, a chimera in my brain, troubles me in my prayer.

He then observed, "So certainly is there nothing, nothing in spiritual things perfect in this world."

The best response I can find for such distraction and lack of letting go is to lessen the struggle. Seated in a quiet place, one need not, I come to sense again, expend considerable energy in some concentrative, psychological, or emotive technique to try to restore inner peace and retain oneself at prayer. Although it may not always be easy to offer, all that is needed is the consent. One consents to be in the way of prayer. One consents to be in the context of Awareness. One consents to be resting in relationship. When troubling or distracting thoughts or ideas bubble up, they may not so much be resisted as let go of. One can do this by repeating a word or phrase. The word (my word is *yes*) is the way of consent. My phrase is repeated from the Psalms: "For God alone my soul waits in silence" (Psalm 62:1).

Other disciplines may help. One may use a rosary or mandala, reflect on one's breathing, walk a labyrinth, or walk at a steady, meditative pace. There are lovely prayers like this one: "O God of peace, who has taught us that in returning and rest we shall be saved, in quietness and in confidence shall be our strength: By the might of your Spirit lift us, we pray, to your presence, where we may be still and know that you are God."

But we need not make an elaborate technique of prayer. If a concern persists, I find it may be best just to let it have its place for a while in the context of the Spirit. If one does not struggle with it, perhaps one may gain a new perspective on the matter. In due course it may grow less substantial and, as it were, lighter. I sometimes imagine myself then letting go of such concerns like helium-filled balloons. They drift off as I return to the *yes* and consent to Presence.

As one rests within this context that is so much greater than one's own awareness, there is bound to be a fresh perspective on self and on one's worries, hopes, and problems. With this perspective may again come acceptance and a healing from the hurts and fears. One is no longer at the center of existence. The *I* may lessen, and grow as the abler self. There may be a sense of peace "which passes all understanding."

Such quieting and lessening of anxiety is sometimes described as detachment. But this resting prayer need not bring on the impassivity of stoicism. The goal, I find, is not to become indifferent to pleasure or pain. The purpose is not to be without care. Rather, the purpose is to develop a different kind of caring: caring in the larger context of divine Awareness of all life, where the pleasure or pain of the self is no longer central.

"Teach us to care and not to care," T .S. Eliot implored in his poem "Ash Wednesday." This petition could be heard to suggest that we are sometimes to be caring and at other times not to care. But the short prayer, I have discovered, asks for a more profound careless caring, or a caring carelessness. In the context of God's Spirit, in a relationship of sharing in the divine empathy and caring, one realizes that this is the ultimate caring that can be offered. Having glimpsed oneself in this perspective, one can become careless in such caring; at the same time, it is this sense of ultimate caring and valuing that enables one to go on caring for others even when it might otherwise seem more sensible to give it up.

Too Deep for Words

In the context of divine Awareness, there are times when the sense of God's presence may become more active. One may feel something of the yearning God's Spirit has, I believe, for our spirits. The Spirit arouses one to desire the God who desires to be in our lives. The Greek word for *spirit* in the Bible is *pneuma*. From it comes a word like *pneumatic*, as in *pneumatic pressure.* This may cause one to think of the divine Spirit as a steady presence—a context like the air around us. The Hebrew word *ruach,* on the other hand, may make one think more often of movement and activity—more like a wind that can be felt, though we do not know where it comes from or where it is going. This is the Spirit Jesus is said to *breathe* on his disciples. "We do not know how to pray as we ought," counseled Paul, but "the Spirit helps us in our weakness." "That very Spirit intercedes with sighs too deep for words. And God, who searches the heart, knows what is the mind of the Spirit, because the Spirit intercedes for the saints according to the will of God" (Romans 8:26–27).

Human words and ideas may falter, perhaps especially when it comes to praying for what one most needs and hopes for. But the Spirit of God, Paul maintained, can interact with the human heart and spirit, helping one to sigh and yearn for what is most wanted. This can be thought of as the Spirit praying with and within. Certainly some days I am tired. Then simple prayers will do. One may be grateful for the praying within, "God's breath in man," to borrow Herbert's description of prayer once again.

I sometimes think of the Spirit interceding in this way when I am praying for others. Often I am not sure what to pray for. Sometimes, as I hold those for whom I am praying in my thoughts, something happens that at first seems rather silly. They begin to levitate in my prayer. They rise up a little off the ground, and I can see them, as it were, from all around. I imagine seeing them not just from the front but from behind and below. They appear rather vulnerable with their feet dangling and jackets flapping in the breeze. One friend, on hearing this, said to me, "If I ever begin to come up off the ground, I'll know that you are praying for me."

What I also imagine is that I am seeing the person whom I am praying for from the perspective of God's Spirit. Although my prayer may have few words, my awareness is able to catch sight of their fragility and sometimes a sense of their greatest need. I imagine this might help align me with the compassion and understanding of God. In that prayer and context I can sometimes feel close to them, able in the spirit to touch them with something of my love and caring.

I am then reminded, too, that we do not pray alone. Others are always praying and sharing in the divine Spirit—often using different words and symbols than I use, if they even use words. It is a form of community—a common or more collective awareness—sometimes called the "communion of saints." At times in such prayer and in the context of Awareness, one may sense an inclusion of the spirits of those who have come and gone before.

On some of our days, prayers may have many words and thoughts. One morning there may be much I want to share with respect to what I hope for and think I need. This wordiness may be true as well of prayers for others and the problems of society and the world. I may wish to articulate gratitude and love. I may want to add a realization of my selfishness and not exercising my potential. I may, then or at other times, find that I wish to meditate and reflect on some theme or idea—perhaps in some cases a scriptural image or story.

There comes a time, however, when I am out of words and thoughts and less concerned to direct the content of prayer and what I am thinking about. I may be content to be more known than knowing. I may be more pleased to be in the divine Presence than to have God present to me. I recall the words of Paul: "Now we see in a mirror, dimly, but then we will see face to face. Now I know only in part; then I will know fully, even as I have been fully known" (1 Corinthians 13:12). I, at best, only partially know and understand myself through my self-awareness. But in the Spirit of God, an awareness may grow of the Awareness that knows me. Then may emerge an enlarged awareness of who I am. A day may come when this enlarging awareness seems to let in, as it were, more light, and offer an *illumination* of the context of Awareness. With this can come ecstasy, that is, the *ek-stasis* of being beyond or even outside of self that may be an encouragement toward greater intimacy in love and exploration of the vast interiority of God's Spirit.

Night Sight

The silence of that interiority can be lovely and awesome, but it can also be frightening. Once, when I had an appointment that called for me to drive through the desert in eastern California, a friend urged me to take part of the trip on old Route 66. Far out in the desert, I left the interstate and drove onto the surprisingly well-preserved two-lane road, at one time a part of the highway that ran from Chicago to Los Angeles. As the interstate veered away, there was no other traffic on the old highway, and I passed an abandoned collection of shacks—decrepit buildings that had been a house, a gas station, and a restaurant in bygone days.

Some miles farther on, I stopped. I walked about thirty yards into the desert, surprised to see all the scrub plants and occasional scurrying critters in what, from a distance, seemed so desolate. For a minute or so, I could hear an occasional pinging from the heat of my car's engine. Then that ceased. There was the sighing of a little wind that gradually faded as well. It was a mite exhilarating to be surrounded by all that silence—perhaps something like the sheer silence in which Elijah found himself.

I thought of trying to rest in that silence, but, although I was in no great hurry, I began to hear the voices of my doubts and fears. The vastness of that silence can seem more like an emptiness, and I suddenly felt very alone. I came to realize again that, no matter what the setting or circumstances, the relationship with the Spirit cannot be sustained by the direction of human awareness. It is at once too intimate and too wholly beyond to be in any way controlled by my efforts. God and the universe are so large. I am so small. Absence can come to seem much greater than Presence.

One may want to believe that this sense of the withdrawal of Spirit can have its role in prayers. Absence may help the heart grow fonder. There is opportunity to realize that what is most desired is a free relationship of love with the Spirit of the God of all creation, and not a relationship that can be possessed and domesticated for one's own ends whenever the prayer button is pushed. But, for whatever reason, few men and women of earnest prayer have not also experienced the absence and the emptiness in the silence.

One hears of this empty silence, and also of darkness, not infrequently in spiritual writings. There is blindness, the dark night, the cloud. One can hope that the purpose of the unknowing and the darkness is to improve true vision. We know how this can happen when one has been out for a long time on a night so dark one can at first barely see ahead. One looks more carefully in the darkness. And the darkness can also bring a greater acceptance and appreciation of the dawn. It is true as well that the loss, even if temporary, of one sense can cause the other senses to be strengthened.

The story of Bartimaeus, the blind beggar (see Mark 10:46–52), is a gospel narrative about such vision. As Jesus passes through Jericho on his way to Jerusalem and his death, a great crowd surrounds him. Many of these people cannot see who he is. This is especially true of some of the astute and otherwise-perceptive religious officials. Their ideas about the way the world can and should be are so strong that they are blind to seeing Jesus' relationship with God. Even the disciples are myopic. Two of them have just asked to have honored positions with Jesus in glory. They are not able to *see* him as the one who came to serve and not to be served. But Bartimaeus, even though he rather unthinkingly and dangerously uses the royal title "Son of David" in calling out to Jesus, does *see* who Jesus is for him. People tell him to be quiet, but he cannot stay silent. Insistently he asks Jesus for mercy. Then, with his healed sight, he is able to follow Jesus "on the way" to Jerusalem and the cross—and finally new life. Through his darkness Bartimaeus has truly come to see.

⊗

There can be purpose, then, in waiting in the darkness, but it can be a waiting and longing. "The meaning," as R. S. Thomas concludes his poem about kneeling in a silent church, "is in the waiting." In one of my own poems, I wrote of

> Some lingering of prayer or song,
> ends of sound in a darkening church,
> a scrap of scripture: for God alone
> my soul awaits, my soul does thirst.
> In the last touches of blues and green

I hold still the book and bare scent
the candles' snuff, waiting too, my prayer
of soul alone in longing bent.

"O God, you are my God," yearns one from long ago. "I seek you"
(Psalm 63:1).

Such waiting and listening for God to be present to us from out of
God's future is, at the least, a form of purgation, a time during which one
must walk by what Saint John of the Cross described as a dark and pure
faith. It is a night of the spirit as well as the senses—an enigmatic night
in which one can know nothing of God. One can only say what God is
not—a context perhaps something like the dark energy of the universe.
One can only wait. T. S. Eliot waited: "I said to my soul, be still, and let
the dark come upon you / Which shall be the darkness of God"; for "the
faith and the love and the hope are all in the waiting."

Any prayer in this waiting is in the context of Awareness, invisible
and silent. Here our being known is unknown to us. Perhaps this is because of all the limits on our ways of knowing in an existence so mysterious to us. Perhaps it is because of fear of God and what we may seem to
lose in relationship. This universal Awareness is, after all, of the God of
the billions of galaxies and years—so awesome and other. It is darkness
because of the unknowable and unapproachable.

One asks again why the God of all that is could not communicate
with our awareness in some clearer way. Perhaps God, who would otherwise fill all in all, voluntarily and mercifully pulls back to make space for
our awareness. The silence and darkness invite the giving of ourselves.
One joins with Jesus in abandonment and in trying faithfully to keep the
questions. The divine nonaction and resting allow the creation to have
some independence and opportunity to be itself so that there can be genuine relationship. Perhaps it is because God is reaching out to us from a
future beyond our grasp of time. Perhaps it is so we will not be overwhelmed and so a gift of relationship may be known: the edge of presence in the absence, the context for the sheer silence, a texture for the
darkness. In the tremor of hope, they become the sacrament. I think of

how there may be a potentiality, an energy and attraction, even in the nothingness, the creative symmetry from which all things come into being. Perhaps it is this that attracts my longing hope so that I may come to *see* that "even the darkness is not dark to you; / the night is as bright as the day, / for darkness is as light to you" (Psalm 139:12).

There is, the mystics claim, light that is too bright for mortal vision. Light itself, we recall, cannot be seen. Spaces can be created in which intense light is shining, but it shines on nothing to catch the eye. The eye itself sees only the dark, as an astronaut looking into the sunlit space sees only darkness.

In the prayer and through the longing, the vast interiority of Awareness, which can at times seem so dark, may again begin to glimmer and even to shine. "I saw Eternity the other night," mused Henry Vaughan. "There is in God (some say) a deep, but dazzling darkness." Vaughan shared this vision with an earlier mystical theologian who also wrote of the darkness:

> The divine dark is none other than the unapproachable light in which God is said to dwell. Although invisible through its dazzling brightness and beyond search because of the outpouring of transcendent brilliance, yet here are found those who are worthy to see and know God. And it is just because they neither see nor know that they come to that which is beyond all seeing and knowing.

Although many people may experience days when their awareness will have an easier sense of God's Spirit, here is a vision of the Spirit well beyond our comprehension. In this Spirit we may be lost and perhaps found. Through our longing for relationship with this Awareness, we may discover at last the loosening of our possessive egos and the awareness of our truer selves, with our place and our rest and peace in the divine compassion where all prayer is simply loving. There is "music heard so deeply," T. S. Eliot inferred, "that it is not heard at all." Or it is heard so closely that we may ask if it is part of us and we are of the music.

Seven ⚭ In Life Beyond

The Peephole Closes

Certainly, if involuntarily, the ego and self-awareness are given up in death. What happens to love and yearning relationship with God's Spirit when we die? What happens to us? What happens to those I love so dearly? What happens to me when comes "unresting death, . . . the sure extinction"?

The questions are as old as humankind. The living ask about their loved ones and themselves. It is hard, however, to get our minds around "the scandal of death." Indeed, we may never do so. We may never be able fully to imagine or admit the coming reality of our personal non-being. At some level we may always be in a state of denial, which, as we have seen, can be a powerful factor in human psychology and artistic work and literature.

It certainly has provided energy for a great deal of religious myth and ritual and for some spectacular buildings. I recall feeling both awed and creepy on my visits to the great pyramids, temples, and burial chambers of Egypt. Many cultures have other monuments to the dead and sometimes elaborate provision for them in the afterlife. Even humble graves sometimes contain a few items that might be of use in a next life.

I remember, when I was a boy, climbing the temple mounds that the Native American Cahokians had built in southern Illinois. The mounds had at least something to do with death. In the museum were beads, tools, and remnants of food that had been buried with their dead.

Yet, however amazing human cognition, reflection, and awareness may be, all thought and awareness appear to be wholly dependent on the hard wiring of the brain and its physical existence. As amazing as it is for a brain with billions of neurons and trillions of synaptic junctures to come into existence, as remarkable as is the capacity for awareness to transcend self and to love, the switchboard operator goes with the switchboard. The software dies along with the hardware.

Few thinking people today are dualists. As was true of the view of existence in the time of the writing of the Hebrew Scriptures, humans are understood to live a wholly integrated bodily life. This does not mean that we must be strictly monistic in our thinking. Mental activity need not be regarded as mere brain activity. We can recognize that all mental events are identical with some physical brain event without reducing all that is mental to the physical. But the dependence of mental activity on brain activity remains. And, after death, all the neurons and synapses, with their form as well as their substance, no longer exist other than in fleeting and fading ways in the awareness and memories of others. People are here, and suddenly they are gone.

It is now understood how the Egyptian mummifiers managed to extract the brain, which would otherwise decay in the skull. A rod was inserted up a nostril of the deceased and stirred vigorously. The resulting soup of brain material was then sucked out. So much for the billions of neurons!

Though some people want to believe that medical technology, perhaps with the aid of cryonics, can one day extend the human life span, the mortality rate remains at one hundred percent. Probably it always will. There were always plenty of what my undertaker grandfather wryly referred to as "my customers." In my role as pastor, I have been with others as they died, a few well-known, others less so. As the woman from Tekoa reminded King David, "We must all die; we are like water spilled on the ground, which cannot be gathered up" (2 Samuel 14:14). More than two thousand years ago, the "ungodly" in the Wisdom of Solomon drove home the point:

> Short and sorrowful is our life,
> and there is no remedy when a life comes to its end,
> and no one has been known to return from Hades.
> For we were born by mere chance,
> and hereafter we shall be as though we had never been,
> for the breath in our nostrils is smoke,
> and reason is a spark kindled by the beating of our hearts;
> when it is extinguished, the body will turn to ashes,
> and the spirit will dissolve like empty air.
>
> (2:1–3)

No life can avoid being overtaken by such dissolution, and our personal "peephole," as Kurt Vonnegut characterizes the individual's vantage point on existence, closes forever with our dying.

Vonnegut also helps us see the comic aspects of our peephole existence. There is so much we are never able to see beyond the peephole; much less can we put our lives into perspective. Big brains we may have, but we are mortal animals, with animal functions and drives. We do some incredibly manic and self-defeating things. We place high valuation on ourselves when we are but one of billions of our race in a whirling arm of one of billions of galaxies. "Life's but a walking shadow," Macbeth tells us, "a poor player / That struts and frets his hour upon the stage / And then is heard no more." How important can we be?

And yet (nor does Vonnegut miss this) our life is tragic, too. Though we are all, at best, bit players in life's drama, we are important to ourselves and to those we love, and they are important to us. As thinking and self-aware beings, we become full of experience and potential. Whether it is an accident or not, each human life is extraordinary in this universe. In the vastness of universal space and amid the huge stretches of otherwise silent time, each consciousness, with all its memories and awareness, is a marvel.

Still, from our perspective, the world ends at our death. Let me say it from my perspective: My peephole will close. Not only is my life then over, but there are no more trees, rivers, birds, friends, or cities. The big dipper and the little dipper, the earth, sun, moon, Shakespeare, and Mozart, all are gone forever. One less mind becomes one less world. There is even a sense in which my mother and father and other dear friends are lost again as my memories of them end. No wonder it is hard not only to think about death but even to conceive of it for oneself.

I Think I Understand

I once did try to think about my death when I wrote a poem called "Scars":

> I think I understand
> how by combustion long or swift and bright
> the eyes and ears, my legs, hands, arms, each gland
> then even teeth, bone at last, from all sight
> are gone to dust and sand.
> Hard although to think
> of being not, and of these my fingers
> that now move and write, and every link
> perhaps saving this, whereby one lingers
> with you, to gravely sink

I know that life will go on, and I do find more than a little consolation in that continuance. There will be sunrises over the lakes of Ontario, fresh springs and crocuses. New lives and stories will come. I love to watch little children at play. Their lives will be in many ways like ours, and perhaps some small measure of what we have done will affect and continue in their lives. I remember on a late winter afternoon standing on the north porch of Princeton's chapel with one of the university's most distinguished scholars. We had just concluded a memorial service for a colleague. He gestured toward Firestone Library across the plaza and, with pride and yet strains of resignation and melancholy in his voice, said, "That is my temple."

I know, too, that death is a natural part of life. It is as natural as life itself and necessary to an ongoing creation. There cannot be new life without death. As earthly time collapses for us and we join with those in the funeral home and all those before and after in the common experience of leaving life, our dying can be seen as a final offering so that others may live. It is even part of life's beauty: each awareness as a mysterious gift that must be returned.

Moreover, neither my life nor anyone else's life is unmitigated blessing. There is much loss and many sorrows. There are hard memories and suffering for ourselves and those for whom we care. Awareness and empathy only increase the scope of these. There is something to look forward to in letting them go. In any event, what would it mean to live this life on and on, not being sure of its value or purpose, and with the sorrows and losses mounting? Surely, at some point, one gets tired of clipping toenails and flossing teeth. Death can be seen as release.

All this is true, though a sharp and stubborn wish for more life rather than nonbeing remains. We lead a life of trouble and tears, it has been observed, and it is over much too soon. Admitting all death's naturalness and all the burden and sorrows of living, and even that there may be no lasting value in human life, there is still an unwillingness to let go. I want to know what will happen to future generations. I want to know what will happen to our hopes for humanity—that we might learn to share more and rid life of severe poverty and human indifference and cruelty. I want to see what new knowledge will be discovered. As a friend and pastor, I have heard a number of people complain that their life at the point of death seems inconclusive to them. They feel a sense of deep loss and a refusal to accept and be consoled. George Steiner again turns to the "unwritten theology" of music. "There is music which conveys both the grave constancy, the finality of death and a certain refusal of that very finality." But however interesting that "certain refusal" and going against the flow may be, they appear as nothing in the face of the ongoing current of death. "Death," Philip Larkin reminds us, "is no different whined at than withstood."

The divine Awareness, we may believe, continues. Perhaps in some way it is lonely in the losing of relationship with us and others. New awarenesses come into being, but it could well seem part of the deep sorrow of creation that these, too, are always disappearing as this earth and then this universe itself go on, eventually to their final end in fire or ice.

Our Stories Saved

Or, as some have guessed, wished for, and intuited in their prayers, are we at least not forgotten? The caring of divine Awareness, it might be hoped, will not let our memories or our stories go. They are instead retained in Awareness and brought together in the tapestry of the great story of all creation. As in some monumental library of books or films, as some vast universal computation, they are saved in God's Spirit. All the stories are needed for the whole story. Perhaps, from some perspective beyond our understanding of time, all the narratives of hurt and wrong, of brave hearts and generous living, are always being told and played as part of the ongoing story of creativity, travail, struggle, suffering, compassion, pageantry, and beauty. Perhaps, in the perspective of this telling, all the incredible size and duration, the profusion and diversity of creation are given their place.

The divine Spirit cruises on, continuing to let be and to observe. Perhaps Awareness might be thought to move, as it were, at or near the speed of light. All that happens in relation to the creative light that lets life be seen slows and is with God forever. Or Awareness may be moving from a future into which all is drawn. Everything of value is preserved in this way—saved by being taken into the Awareness and the compassion of God. The story is retold and the tapestry rewoven seeking new patterns and reconciliation—a place for all, even all the wounds.

In my poem "Scars," I remembered my falling out of the tree, when Lefty socked me, when a problem in my lung caused me to cough up blood, and the back operation—broken bones and many cuts and stitches. I thought, too, of other kinds of hurts and wounds, not only mine but those of others. I alluded, as well, to the wounding Jacob received after wrestling with God, to my own God-wrestling, and to the

scars of Jesus. What happens to our scars?
 Yet still I think, would know
what happens to the scars I feel, I've earned:
the door, then shovel crossed on a child's brow;
more by sport and in a paned glass door turned
 by a little girl, oh!
 So I think of mother,
phone again ringing, nearly once a year,
some cut, or fracture when for her brother
sister shouting, he fell so far, so near
 to breaking heart of her.
 As I think, too, of scars
engraved on the bone of leg and arm,
how a cheekbone cracking in a fight mars
now not at all (I laugh), nor the nose harmed.
 All past now, all honors.
 I think how it went on:
of one of these fingers jaggedly snared,
and finer lines of healing incision,
gall bladder gone, back, shoulder, lung repaired.
 Yes! quite a collection!
 They must, I think, stand, too,
for colder wounds, acts that seemed unfeeling,
undone and done, sharp words, as most I rue,
my cuts to others, for whose scars healing,
 too, I will pray anew.
 Not least I think of times
trying, trying to hunger and vying
for some modicum of fairness, those signs
for others, of just hands, a heart sharing,
 caring against our crimes,
 Which has me think of night
long wrestling with the one not letting go,
who for some yet veiling love and its rite

> of wounds that may heal sends me limping so
>   into the breaking light.
>   Then I can but think well
> of holes hammered in palms and feet, his side,
> and, why not, too? as saw slipped or chisel
> while like us learning, so that when he died,
>   they after knew love still.

And then I concluded in hope and prayer:

> I think some way they're laid
> in days to come, if not on our new selves.
>   Then in that life with whom as we are made
> hurts, known and knelled, are so reformed it tells
>   that they with we are saved.

The possibility of our lives, our scars, and our stories being saved in the divine Awareness is a glorious intuition. It is a dream substantiated for some—and perhaps in different ways for many—by their experience of the Spirit of God in a relationship marked by affirmation and hope. There we are known and know ourselves in this perspective. No longer needing or wanting to be at life's center, we yet are not lost sight of for who we are and have been. *I know your name; I will not forget you and your awareness*, whispers God's Spirit. *I will not let you go.* Such an intuition and such a hope are at the edge of the human horizon.

Continuing in Awareness

Dare I ask what more it might mean for the memory of the relationship with our awareness to be held in divine Awareness? What might it mean for our awareness to continue to participate in this way in the Awareness of God?

Our awareness, we recall, includes an awareness of all that we are: our mind with our brain and body. We are aware of our conscious and unconscious selves, our thoughts and feelings, memories and stories, who we are and have been and may be. We are aware of our capacity to think beyond ourselves and in this sense to begin to transcend self. We may believe that in this we are in the *image* of God and have a relationship with divine Awareness.

What might it mean for this awareness to be kept in relationship by the Spirit who has let us and all life be? Might it be that our awareness also in some way continues? Some theologians say that it is selfish and even idolatrous to ask such a question. Only God lives on. But it does not feel like selfishness. It feels more like love.

This could not be other than a gift of acceptance and caring by divine Awareness. It would not, as Paul intuited, be the same body we have known. It would be a different kind of life, but perhaps not unrelated to the physical body included now in our awareness. Even in this life, after all, our continuing being is more a matter of form than the specific matter that keeps changing.

At one point in his ruminations, Paul thought of human beings becoming, as it were, unclothed in death—leaving this mortal "tent" (see 2 Corinthians 5:1–4). But, he hoped, we would not be left naked. We would be found in a new kind of clothing. With this hope in mind, I wrote in "Scars":

> In faith one thinks, one hopes
> Of that other tent, of some reclothing,
> That not in nakedness, but with new tropes
> Of sight and voice, and ourselves emerging,
> All dressed in shining coats.

In more traditional religious language, this essential or abler self of our awareness might be called the soul. And heaven we would imagine not so much in terms of place but as relationship—a continuing relationship with divine Awareness, and with others in this relationship, that can already be begun and appreciated in mortal life. This increased and ongoing awareness and Awareness would be the *point* in a creation that might otherwise seem ultimately pointless.

With any such thoughts, one is now well beyond the horizon of our understanding. We are beyond even our dreams, though not our hoping. That hope exists in the context of a relationship with the Spirit of all life, and I will confess, though I feel shy about doing so, that I have had a kind of vision. Perhaps I might better call it an intuition that seems to draw me outside my being. Indeed, I do not know what to call it. But I sense some greater blending of awarenesses. There is a further letting go of ego and even of identity, but mostly of the self-serving kind. The gain in communion with others, of which our caring now is only a foretaste, more than compensates. Here are forgiveness, understanding, and healing. I imagine laughter and forms of music. Awarenesses flutter about. It seems like dancing.

My critical and questioning mind exclaims, *How impossible! You are only imagining what you vainly hope might be.* And then the intuition returns. However much I may doubt, and however much I at times find these qualities absent in larger contexts, there it remains as part of my experience of a relationship in which I find acceptance and caring—a sharing of the divine imagination of what life will be.

For Christians the hope is also glimpsed in Jesus, whose Spirit, Christians believe, continues to live in and with the Spirit of God. We may believe that he, in a unique way, lived in the image of God, but that we all, through our awareness, also have that image. In this sense he was once described as "a forerunner on our behalf" (Hebrews 6:20). Another of the New Testament writers held out the faith that "what we will be has not yet been revealed. What we do know is this: when he is revealed, we will be like him" (1 John 3:2).

The hope that the creation and our humanity are still unfinished, and that God is God of the yet-to-be-determined future of possibilities, can be set forth in words that paraphrase a vision first sketched by Paul:

> I believe that what we suffer now will be seen in new light
> when compared to all that God intends for us. The creation,
> still unfinished, longs in expectation for the children of God
> to know the fullness of life. A day will come when the limi-

tations of decay will be overcome. Now it is as though the whole creation is straining in the pangs of birth, and we, too, are caught up in the struggling. But we have been given a taste of the Spirit of all life and with it hope in our weakness. Though our vision is limited, and we do not even know what words to use for our prayer, the Spirit moves deep within us.

Present Hope

The significance of any faith like this means at least as much for present life as for the future. The life that I live now is profoundly affected by this hope. Because in the divine perspective, all that has turned to the beauty of love's compassion is never lost, all also matters now. Because goodness will continue to be treasured, it becomes of even more value to seek now to live by the Spirit's ways. It becomes still more important to enlarge awareness and to strive against the forces that would dehumanize others and inhibit opportunities for their awareness to grow in the image of God. Of greater consequence become efforts to make place for others, to share compassion, to live with empathy, kindness, gentleness, and generosity. The events of this life would then not just be over and forever gone but will become parts of our living future.

The DC-10 seemed to land too fast and, for whatever reason, had trouble slowing. In the snowscape alongside the runway, I saw one, two, then three of the turnoffs hurtle by. There wasn't a sound on the plane. I saw the last of the runway go, and there followed a series of sharp bumps. My prayer was short and primitive.

In these and other prime moments of our lives, hope and prayer are sharpened. Is our awareness alone in the world? Is our awareness related to some fundamental aspect of universal life? What might that relationship be like? Does it involve any care for what happens to us and others? Why is there so much suffering and wrong? Does life have any value and meaning, any enduring beauty? What happens to our awareness at death?

A faith that responds, "Even though I walk through the valley of the shadow of death . . . you are with me" trusts that our awareness continues to be valued in God's. God, then, as the saying goes, isn't finished with us yet. God is not finished with all of God's hope. Indeed, by this hope we may only have begun to be the people the Spirit of God wishes us to be. But in the context of the divine Awareness of all life, we may believe that we have begun, and, in this Spirit, find a sense of questing adventure for now and all that is to be.

Notes for Further Reading

As I have kept the questions over the years, I have been in dialogue with a number of authors as well as teachers, students, colleagues, and friends. Here are references to reading pertinent to *Keeping the Questions* that may be helpful for further exploration and thought.

Preface

Frederick Buechner has long been one of the explorers of life's questions. He describes most theology as essentially autobiographical in *The Alphabet of Grace* (1970; repr. San Francisco: HarperSanFrancisco, 1989).

One • With Self Aware

There have been numerous recent investigations into how the brain functions, aided by computers and scanning technology. The 1990s were even called "the decade of the brain." Philosophers and others continue to reflect on the brain-mind relationship and on the nature and significance of consciousness and awareness. Among the books are Colin McGinn, *The Mysterious Flame: Conscious Minds in a Material World* (New York: Basic Books, 1999); Steven Pinker, *How the Mind Works* (New

York: W. W. Norton, 1997); Steven Rose, ed., *From Brains to Consciousness? Essays on the New Sciences of the Mind* (Princeton, NJ: Princeton University Press, 1998); and Gerald M. Edelman and Giulio Tononi, *A Universe of Consciousness: How Matter Becomes Imagination* (New York: Basic Books, 2000). For more on how consciousness may have developed, note *God, Humanity and the Cosmos: A Textbook in Science and Religion*, by Christopher Southgate and other contributors (Harrisburg, PA: Trinity Press International, 1999), especially pages 163–184.

In her poetry Emily Dickinson often reflected on the capacities and whims of awareness. Her work is available in numerous editions. On her beliefs and questions, see Roger Lundin, *Emily Dickinson and the Art of Belief* (Grand Rapids, MI: Eerdmans, 2nd ed. 2004).

Helen Keller tells of her world and experiences in *The Story of My Life: The Restored Classic*, edited by Roger Shattuck (New York: W.W. Norton, 2004).

In his *Oneself and Another*, translated by Kathleen Blamey (Chicago: University of Chicago Press, 1992), Paul Ricoeur muses on the mysteries of personhood and the narrative identity of the self.

Among the philosophers and sociobiologists one might be in dialogue with about human nature and any "freedom" in life are Edward O. Wilson, for example, *On Human Nature* (Cambridge, MA: Harvard University Press, 1978; the edition published in 2004 includes a new preface). Also see Richard Dawkins, *The Selfish Gene* (Oxford, England: Oxford University Press, 1989). Note Stephen Jay Gould, *Rocks of Ages: Science and Religion in the Fullness of Life* (New York: Ballantine Books, 1999), and compare Warren S. Brown, Nancey Murphy, and H. Newton Maloney, *Whatever Happened to the Soul? Scientific and Theological Portraits of Human Nature* (Minneapolis: Fortress Press, 1998).

Two • In a Real World

Gerard Manley Hopkins sought God in the world of nature as well as the spirit. The "fire-folk sitting in the air" is from his poem "The Starlight Night," and, later in the chapter, "like shining from shook foil" and the Holy Ghost brooding with "ah! Bright wings" from "God's Grandeur," in *Gerard Manley Hopkins: The Major Works*, edited by Catherine Phillips (Oxford, England: Oxford University Press, 1986; rev. ed. 2002). W. B. Yeats alludes to the dance and the dancer in his poem "Among School Children," in *The Collected Poems of W. B. Yeats*, 2nd rev. ed., edited by Richard J. Finneran (1933; repr. New York: Scribner, 1996). The "infinite in all directions" observation of Emil Wiechert is quoted by Freeman J. Dyson and used for the title of his *Infinite in All Directions* (New York: Harper and Row, 1988). Note also Dyson's *Imagined Worlds* (Cambridge, MA: Harvard University Press, 1997). A host of other books, many of them with splendid titles, seek to probe the physics of our world. Among those that have influenced the questioning and thoughts of this chapter are *The Elegant Universe: Superstrings, Hidden Dimensions, and the Quest for the Ultimate Theory,* by Brian Greene (New York: W. W. Norton, 1999), and now his *The Fabric of the Cosmos: Space, Time and the Texture of Reality* (New York: Knopf, 2004); *The Fire in the Equations: Science, Religion and the Search for God,* by Kitty Ferguson (1994; repr. West Conshohocken, PA: Templeton Foundation Press, 2004); *A Hole in the Universe: How Science Peered Over the Edge of the Universe and Found Everything,* by K. C. Cole (New York: Harcourt, 2001); *Creation Revisited,* by Peter W. Atkins (New York: W. H. Freeman, 1992); *God, Chance and Necessity,* by Keith Ward (Oxford: Oneworld, 1996); *Quintessence: The Mystery of the Missing Mass in the Universe,* by Lawrence Krauss (New York: Basic Books, 2000); *Fire in the Mind: Science, Faith and the Search for Order,* by George Johnson (New York: Vintage Books, 1996); *Soul: God, Self, and the New Cosmology,* by Angela Tilby (New York: Doubleday, 1995); *God and Contemporary Science,* by Philip D. Clayton (Grand Rapids, MI: Eerdmans, 1997); *Quarks, Chaos and Christianity: Questions to Science and Religion,* by John Polkinghorne (New York: Crossroad, 1999); *God, Creation and Contemporary Physics,* by Mark William Worthing (Minneapolis: Fortress Press, 1996); *Religion in an Age of Science,* by Ian G. Barbour (San Francisco: Harper and Row, 1990); *Theology for a Scientific Age: Being and Becoming—Natural, Divine and Human,* by Arthur Peacocke (Minneapolis: Fortress Press, 1993); *The Emperor's New Mind: Concerning Computers, Minds and the Laws of*

Physics, by Roger Penrose (Oxford, England: Oxford University Press: 1989; reprinted with new preface, 1999).

Renowned physicist and teacher for many years at Princeton, John Archibald Wheeler has become a kind of guru of physics, and one enjoys his stories as well as the science of *Geons, Black Holes and Quantum Foam,* with Kenneth Ford (New York: W. W. Norton, 1998), and *At Home in the Universe* (New York: Springer-Verlag, 1996). There is also an interview with Wheeler in *The Ghost in the Atom,* edited by P. C. W. Davies and J. R. Brown (Cambridge, England: Cambridge University Press, 1986).

M. Mitchel Waldrop writes on *Complexity: The Emerging Science on the Edge of Order and Chaos* (New York: Simon and Schuster, 1992), as do Peter Coveney and Roger Highfield in *Frontiers of Complexity: The Search for Order in a Chaotic World* (New York: Ballantine Books, 1995). On the wonder and mystery of the properties of light and perception, note *Catching the Light: The Entwined History of Light and Mind,* by Arthur Zajonc (Oxford, England: Oxford University Press, 1995). With thoughts on the mental dimensions of the universe, including discussions of the work of James Jeans and Erwin Schroedinger, confer *Quantum Questions: Mystical Writings of the World's Great Physicists,* edited by Ken Wilber (Boston: Shambhala, 2001), and also *The Mind of God: The Scientific Basis for a Rational World,* by Paul Davies (New York: Simon and Schuster, 1992).

Francis Thompson intuited "all things . . . linked are" in "Mistress of Vision," found in *The Complete Poems of Francis Thompson* (New York: Random House, n.d.). George Steiner probes for life's coherencies in *Real Presences* (Chicago: University of Chicago Press, 1989). Wallace Stevens, another who probes life's conjunctions and mysteries, mused on our living in the description of a place in a letter of April 4, 1945, to his friend Henry Church in *Letters of Wallace Stevens,* edited by Holly Stevens (New York: Knopf, 1966). The thought led to his poem "Description Without Place." Henry Moore reflected on artists being religious in his *Henry Moore: Writings and Conversations,* edited by Alan G. Wilkinson (Berkeley, CA: University of California Press, 2002).

Three • In Spirit and Spirit

John V. Taylor's significant study of the Holy Spirit was first published in 1972 by SCM Press in England: *The Go-Between God: The Holy Spirit and Christian Mission* (Philadelphia: Fortress Press, 1973).

Richard of St. Victor reflected on searching of the self and spirit in *The Mystical Ark*, in the translation of Grover A. Zinn, *Richard of St. Victor: The Twelve Patriarchs, The Mystical Ark, Book Three of the Trinity* (New York: Paulist Press, 1979). The dynamic of searching for God through one's inmost soul and spirit was strongly influenced, mediated through Augustine's similar reflections, by neo-Platonic thought. Anthony Bloom meditated in like manner in *Beginning to Pray* (New York: Paulist Press, 1970). Thomas Merton wrote often of the experience of spirit and God in, for instance, *Contemplative Prayer* (New York: Herder and Herder, 1969) and, as in the quotation in this chapter, in *The Dublin Review* (London: Burns amd Oates, 1949), as quoted by Kenneth Leech in *Soul Friend* (San Francisco: Harper, 1977). See also my *Coming Together in the Spirit: A New Approach to Christian Community* (Cincinnati: Forward Movement, 1980). Paul Tillich thought similarly in the terms of his more existentialist and eclectic theology in *The Theology of Culture* (New York: Oxford University Press, 1959). *The Cloud of Unknowing* can be read in the translation by Clifton Wolters, *The Cloud of Unknowing and Other Works* (New York: Penguin Books, 1978), and Meister Eckhart in *Meister Eckhart: A Modern Translation,* by R. B. Blakney, first published in 1941 (New York: Harper and Brothers). Baron Friedrich von Hügel, a modernist Roman Catholic lay thinker much interested in science, history, and prayer, presented the life and thought of Catherine of Genoa (as well as Eckhart and others) and his own understanding of the relation of the divine and human spirits in his two volume *The Mystical Element of Religion as Studied in Saint Catherine of Genoa and her Friends* (New York: E. P. Dutton and Company, 1923).

N. Ross Reat and Edmund F. Perry write on commonalities among the world's religions in *A World Theology: The Central Spiritual Reality of Humankind* (Cambridge, England: Cambridge University Press, 1991), and Matthew Fox offers a compendium of references to the Spirit and spiritual quotations from many faiths in *One River, Many Wells: Wisdom Springing from Global Faiths* (New York: Tarcher/Putnam, 2000). Diana L. Eck tells of "The Fire and Freedom of the Spirit" in her chapter "The Breath of God," in *Encountering God: A Spiritual Journey from Bozeman to Banaras* (Boston: Beacon Press, 1993). The Upanishads may be read in the translation by Juan Mascaró (Baltimore: Penguin, 1965) and the Bhagavad-Gita in the translation by Barbara Stoler Miller (New York: Bantam Books, 1986).

With the thousands of books about Jesus, I have found myself in recent years in dialogue with John P. Meier, who has completed three volumes of *A Marginal Jew: Rethinking the Historical Jesus* (New York: Doubleday, 1991–2001); with the several books of N. T. Wright, including *The Challenge of Jesus: Rediscovering Who Jesus Was and Is* (Downers Grove, IL: InterVarsity Press, 1999); and with Marcus Borg's *Meeting Jesus Again for the First Time: The Historical Jesus and the Heart of Contemporary Faith* (San Francisco: HarperCollins, 1995). I have written of Jesus in *God's Parable* (Philadelphia: Westminster Press, 1975); *Jesus: The Human Life of God* (Cincinnati: Forward Movement, 1987); and *The Son of Man in Myth and History* (Philadelphia: Westminster Press, 1967). On the healing stories and parables, see my *Power in Weakness: New Hearing for Gospel Stories of Healing and Discipleship* (Philadelphia: Fortress Press, 1983) and *Many Things in Parables: Extravagant Stories of New Community* (Philadelphia: Fortress Press, 1988). In *The People Called: The Growth of Community in the Bible* (Louisville, KY: Westminster John Knox Press, 2001), Paul D. Hanson stresses the worship of God both righteous and merciful throughout the Bible. On the God of Judaism who suffers, see Abraham Joshua Heschel in *The Prophets* (New York: Harper & Row, 1969). In his 1963 book *Honest to God* (Philadelphia: Westminster Press), Bishop John A. T. Robinson wrote on what some regarded as untraditional ways of thinking about God's presence in the world and about the ministry and role of Jesus. His efforts to bring to the attention of others the thinking of theologians like Rudolph Bultmann, Dietrich Bonhoeffer, and Paul Tillich caused something of a sensation at the time. His musings may seem tamer, though still worth pondering, today. Robinson wrote of insights into God's character and presence that may be defined by but not confined to Jesus.

One may read more of the thirteenth-century poet Maulana Jalal al-Din Rumi in *The Sufi Path of Love: The Spiritual Teachings of Rumi*, translated by William C. Chittick (Albany, NY: State University of New York Press, 1983).

Four • In the Suffering

Charles Darwin's penetrating insights into the processes of evolution caused him to struggle with his own understanding of God and divine providence. Darwinism and more advanced evolutionary understandings have been a challenge to many thoughtful believers. In *God After Darwin: A Theology of Evolution* (Boulder, CO: Westview Press, 2000), John F. Haught offers a more positive assessment of the compatibility of evolutionary biology and faith in a creative God of self-giving love. The philosopher, theologian, and naturalist Holmes Rolston III meditates profoundly on evolution and the values of human life in *Genes, Genesis and God: Values and Their Origins in Natural and Human History* (New York: Cambridge University Press, 1999), from which comes his affirmation at the end of this chapter. I have also been well instructed and provoked to further thought by his *Science and Religion: A Critical Survey* (New York: Random House, 1987).

"Praise" and "The Ponds" can be found in *House of Light: Poems by Mary Oliver* (Boston: Beacon Press, 1990). John Polkinghorne reflects on God's risk of self-limitation in creation in *The Faith of a Physicist: Reflections of a Bottom-Up Thinker* (Princeton, NJ: Princeton University Press, 1994). Jack Miles meditates on how Jesus' death may be read as a story about the limit's of God's power in the face of evil and death in *Christ: A Crisis in the Life of God* (New York: Random House, 2002). How Woody Allen has loved his inimitable way of posing the big questions! His aside on God's underachievement comes after all the misdirected love and mayhem of *Love and Death* (1975).

R. S. Thomas commented on George Herbert's quarrel with God in his introduction to *A Choice of George Herbert's Verse* (London: Faber, 1967). "Artillerie," "Prayer (I)," which tells of God's breath in man, and other of Herbert's poems I have engaged in these chapters may be read in *The Country Parson, The Temple*, edited by John N. Wall Jr. (New York: Paulist Press, 1981). On importunity in Donne's poems and prayers, see "With Holy Importunity and Pious Impudency: John Donne's Attempts to Provoke Election," in *The Journal of the Rocky Mountain Medieval and Renaissance Association*, 13 (1992).

Elie Wiesel has written many stories and reflections searching for hope and some beauty in life in the aftermath of the Shoah, here in a prayer from *One Generation After* (New York: Random House, 1970). Herbert's poem that begins "My heart did heave . . ." is titled "Affliction (III)." Many a poet, philosopher, and theologian has wrestled with the problem of suffering and evil and what this might tell us of life and of God. Jürgen Moltmann does so in *The Crucified God: The Cross of Christ as the Foundation and Criticism of Christian Theology*, translated by R. A. Wilson and John Bowden (London: SCM Press, 1974). Note also his *The Spirit of Life: A Universal Affirmation*, translated by Margaret Kohl (Minneapolis: Fortress Press, 1992). The issues are at the heart of W. H. Vanstone's *The Risk of Love* (New York: Oxford University Press, 1978), in which he reflected on God as life's Companion; in Paul S. Fiddes's *The Creative Suffering of God* (New York: Oxford University Press, 1988); and in Marilyn McCord Adams's *Horrendous Evils and the Goodness of God* (Ithaca, NY: Cornell University Press, 1999). From personal experience Dietrich Bonhoeffer knew *The Cost of Discipleship*, translated by R. H. Fuller (New York: Macmillan, 1959). "Christians and Others" was written in prison and is found in *The Prison Poems of Dietrich Bonhoeffer: A New Translation and Commentary*, translated by Edwin Robertson (Guildford, Surrey, England: Eagle, 1998). See also his *Letters and Papers from Prison: The Enlarged Edition*, edited by Eberhard Bethge (London: SCM Press, 1971).

Dag Hammarskjöld's reflections were published as *Markings*, translated by Leif Sjöberg and W. H. Auden (New York: Knopf, 1964). "The Revival" ("the lilies of his love"), "The Night" (in chapter 6), and other poems of the seventeenth-century poet Henry Vaughan are collected in *Henry Vaughan: The Complete Poems*, edited by Alan Rudrum (New Haven, CT: Yale University Press, 1981).

Five • While Knowing Ourselves

An earlier version of the prayer—now song and hymn—to see (or know) the Lord more clearly, love more dearly, and follow more nearly is attributed to Richard, Bishop of Chichester, in mid-thirteenth-century England. Augustine's *Confessions*, which may be read in the translation by Henry Chadwick (Oxford: Oxford University Press, 1991), continues to be the classic spiritual autobiography and struggle to understand the self and its motivations, though always with its focus on God. Among his first words are "You have made us for yourself, and our heart is restless until it rests in you," referred to in chapter 6. Blaise Pascal was another insightful mediator on the human condition. In his *Pensées* (here in my translation; see the French with English version of Martin Turnell, London: Harvill Press, 1962), he reflected on humanity caught between grandeur and misery, often trying to escape this condition through distractions. Edna St. Vincent Millay pictured the feathering of our nests in her poem "Bobolink," in *The Buck in the Snow and Other Poems* (New York: Harper and Brothers, 1928).

Franklin Roosevelt set forth the test of progress as providing enough for those who have too little in his Second Inaugural Address of 1936 in the midst of the great depression. Ernest Becker reflected on death from psychological and philosophical perspectives in *The Denial of Death* (New York: Free Press, 1973). Philip Larkin's "Aubade" is in *Philip Larkin: Collected Poems*, edited by Anthony Thwaite (New York: Farrar, Strauss and Giroux, 2004).

I have thought more about whether the golden rule involves true altruism in "The Golden Rule—Is It Enough?" in *Outrage and Hope: A Bishop's Reflections in Times of Change and Challenge* (Valley Forge, PA.: Trinity Press International, 1996). "If I am not for myself, who will be? But, if I am only for myself, who am I?" is attributed to the first-century (CE) Rabbi Hillel and is found in the Talmud's *Pirke Avot,* or *Sayings of the Fathers.* The saying concludes, "And, if not now, when?"

C. S. Lewis was extraordinary in his many interests and gifts for storytelling, literary criticism, and theology. *The Screwtape Letters* (New York: Macmillan, 1943), mentioned in the next chapter, provides often humorous but sharp critique of the pitfalls of the life of prayer and efforts at Christian betterment. The death of the wife he married late in life brought great sorrow and deeper questions to his faith. He wrote of sharing in the beauty in his essay "The Weight of Glory" in *The Weight of Glory and Other Addresses* (New York: Macmillan, 1949). Versions of a story of a gem that is shared have been told by Anthony de Mello, for instance, "The Diamond," in *The Song of the Bird* (Garden City, NY: Image Books, 1982).

Six • While Restless and Resting

In *Waiting for God*, translated by Emma Craufurd (New York: G. P. Putnam, 1951), Simone Weil told of her expectant waiting for God's presence and of her belief that, while this could be experienced in the Church, for her it had to be realized outside what she saw as those consolations.

As a young man, I was once able to talk with Robert Frost, who had a philosophical and sometimes prickly relationship with faith at best, while yet he wondered and explored in his often arch, sometimes amused voice, touched with pity. His poem "The Master Speed" is in *The Poetry of Robert Frost: The Collected Poems, Complete and Unabridged*, edited by Edward Connery Lathem (New York: Holt, Rinehart and Winston, 1969). Wendell Berry, attentive storyteller and poet of nature and the soul, reflects on "the mind that comes to rest" in his *Sabbaths* (San Francisco: North Point Press, 1987).

John Donne's comic description of the distractions of prayer is from a sermon (on John 11:21) preached at the funerals (!) of Sir William Cockayne, Knight, Alderman of London, on December 12, 1626, which is found in volume 7 of *Sermons of John Donne*, edited by George R. Potter and Evelyn M. Simpson (Berkeley, CA: University of California Press, 1953–1962). Many are the books on prayer. I have benefited from contributions like M. Basil Pennington's *Centering Prayer: Renewing an Ancient Christian Prayer Form* (Garden City, NY: Image Books, 1980) and John Koenig's *Rediscovering New Testament Prayer: Boldness and Blessing in the Name of Jesus* (New York: Harper, 1992). Thomas Keating, in *Open Mind, Open Heart: The Contemplative Dimension of the Gospel*

(Amity, NY: Amity House, 1986) and *The Human Condition: Contemplation and Transformation* (New York: Paulist Press, 1999), teaches about prayer and the self-serving habits of the false self.

R. S. Thomas was a Welsh priest and poet who made art of the austerities of the life of the spirit. His poem "Kneeling" is in *R. S. Thomas: Selected Poems* (New York: Phoenix House, 2003). T. S. Eliot's imaginings of the divine dark, dispossession, and the waiting in "East Coker," along with "the music heard so deeply" of "The Dry Salvages," are from "The Four Quartets." This and his "Ash Wednesday" are in *The Complete Poems and Plays: 1909–1935* (New York: Harcourt, Brace, 1952).

In sixteenth-century Spain, John of the Cross was a younger friend and sometimes coworker with Teresa of Ávila in the monastic life. He knew the value of spiritual companionship as well as the soul's dark night of faith. *The Collected Works of St. John of the Cross* are translated by Kieran Kavanaugh and Otilio Rodriguez (Washington, DC: ICS Publications, rev. 1991). The "negative theology" of the vision of the divine dark and its "unapproachable light" (see 1 Timothy 6:16) is attributed to a figure known as Dionysius the Areopagite, whose writings have generated a considerable amount of controversy as to both their origins and their value for orthodox teaching. The more authentic writings (others were later attributed to him) seem to go back to an otherwise anonymous theologian of the fifth century under neo-Platonic influence, whose thought would, in turn, have considerable influence on mystics and theologians in the late medieval period. This passage, in something of my own translation, is from "A Letter to Dortheus, a minister," which can be read in *The Divine Names and Mystical Theology,* by Pseudo-Dionysius the Areopagite, and translated by John D. Jones (Milwaukee: Marquette University Press, 1980).

Seven • In Life Beyond

The peepholes of several of Kurt Vonnegut's characters close in *Deadeye Dick* (New York: Dell Publishing, 1985).